Meal Prep

The ultimate guide to meal prep
And great recipes helps you
To lose weight FASTTTTTTT

Johnny Markus

© 2017

Additionally, the information in the following pages is intended only for informational purposes and should thus be thought of as universal. As befitting its nature, it is presented without assurance regarding its prolonged validity or interim quality. Trademarks mentioned are done without written consent and can in no way be considered an endorsement from the trademark holder.

Table of Contents

Introduction

No one enjoys preparing an evening meal in a cluttered kitchen, especially at the end of a tiring day. So you should take the time to put your meal preparation area in order with the right kitchen organizers. Doing so will make life much easier. You don't want to be looking for a clear space on the counter or stove top to rest your hot pot lid or cooking spoon. The Lid and Spoon Rest is the perfect spot for those items and it's always ready to help you out. One half of this storage tool is a handy spoon rest. It has a slight bowl shape so even the messiest cooking spoon won't drip onto your counter. The other half of the tool holds your pot or pan lid in an upright position, making it easy to set aside and easy to grab, too. The unit is made of stainless steel with rubber feet so it won't scratch your counter...and it will stay in place while you're using it.

Protect your kitchen counter from knives and stains by using a prep board. One of the nicest is the Prep Board with Angled Sides. Made of end grain acacia wood, this is a durable as well as lovely kitchen preparation accessory. Chop all your veggies and fruit on this convenient surface, wash it in hot, soapy water and then use it as a handsome tray. Do you enjoy frying foods but hate having to drag out several different containers to hold your flour, egg, bread crumbs and other ingredients? Take a look at the Breading Tray Set. This three-section tray is perfect for holding everything you need. Place your ingredients in the order you plan to use them, and you'll find that preparing breaded foods is simpler-and less messy-than ever. The three compartments detach for easy hand washing, and then they stack in a small area, saving you something else important: storage space.

When you're done with your prep work, simply open the drawer or cabinet and lift the Scrap Trap away to the trash can. Empty it into the trash and then place it directly into your dishwasher. Made of durable white plastic, it holds up to two quarts of almost anything you can throw at it. Everyone needs to keep a towel handy when preparing food. But who wants to toss it on the counter where it can pick up bits of food or soak up liquids, rendering it almost useless when it comes time to dry your hands? The Over Drawer Towel Holder is the key to keeping your kitchen towels handy but clean. The holder fits over the top of any cabinet door, so you can place it wherever you need to keep a towel within convenient reach. Made of brushed stainless steel, it also looks bright and contemporary in any kitchen. These are just a few of the handy organizers that will keep your meal prep area in order. You'll appreciate them so much that you'll find cooking the pleasant and productive task it's meant to be.

What is meal prepping?

If you're not really familiar with the term, meal prepping refers to planning and prepping your meals in advance. This implies cooking items in a bulk and eating leftovers. This practice of meal prepping is beneficial not only for your health but budget too.

Many people have recognized the benefits of meal prepping and it became extremely popular in saving time and eating healthy. Preparing foods for an entire week has become an inseparable part of weight-loss programs such as Weight Watchers or Ketogenic Diet. The reason is simple; meal prepping can help you stick with your diet plan and therefore achieve your weight loss goals!

Meal Prep Benefits

Dinner preparing is prevalent because of the various advantages it offers. Is it accurate to say that you are pondering doing likewise? Indeed, in case you're uncertain then the accompanying advantages will inspire you to begin doing as such!

Saves time – This is the most vital advantage of feast preparing. How often have you needed to begin eating more hearty meal, and if you didn't have enough time to make it yourself, so you wound up requesting a pizza? Yes, that happens to every one of us. Dinner preparing permits you to eat solid suppers consistently, without cooking each day after work.

Less wasted food – Did you realize that Americans squander around 40% of food and it's for the most part in family units and ranches? On the off chance that you consider the cost of nourishment you get ready, then include the amount you squander a week after week, month to month, and yearly premise, then you can securely finish up this is terrible for your financial plan and for the earth also. Dinner preparing is about part control, picking the perfect measure of fixings, and eating all nourishments from the supper arrange consistently.

Healthier eating - Did you realize that Americans squander around 40% of food and it's generally in family units and ranches? In the event that you consider the cost of nourishment you get ready, then include the amount you squander a week after week, month to month, and yearly premise, then you can securely finish up this is terrible for your financial plan and for the earth too. Feast preparing is about part control, picking the appropriate measure of fixings, and eating all nourishments from the supper arrange consistently.

Stress relief - you know about this situation; you're having a terrible day at work and you return home just to put on something else (now and again not by any means that) and go to the kitchen to begin cooking for your family. Worry from work combined with depletion and dissatisfaction over what to cook can be excessive. Don't you merit some an opportunity to unwind? Obviously, you do. That is the reason dinner preparing is perfect for individuals who are in a hurry. When you're home from work you don't need to stress over what to cook since you have officially arranged what to eat consistently. Presently, you can simply take your most loved book and read while tasting on some lemonade. Isn't that a superior situation?

Avoids "Mom, what are we going to eat?" questions – On the off chance that you have children, then you most likely need to answer this question each and every day. Here and there you know the appropriate response and say it and here and there you don't. In the last case, your youngster continues approaching what's for supper until you make sense of it. Let's be honest: kids don't surrender. While preparing dinners for the week, you can simply make a feast plan and post it onto an ice chest. That way, your children will dependably comprehend what's for lunch or supper, and you'll stay away from your "top choice" question.

Meal Prepping Essentials

In the previous chapter, we looked at the meaning and importance of meal prepping. In this chapter, we will look at the essentials of meal prepping.

When it comes to prepping for a meal, you will need a few basic items that are as follows:

Containers

First, you will require containers in which to place the prepped ingredients. Containers can be of any shape and size depending on your needs. If you are prepping for a big family then choose large containers that can hold a lot more of the ingredients. It would be ideal to buy containers that are microwave safe. Ensure that all the containers are BPA free. Try to have separate containers for vegetables and meats as mixing them can cause the flavors to mingle and interfere with the taste of the meal. If you are keen on prepping several meals at a time, then consider buying the containers at wholesale stores that provide you with discounts. But try not to compromise on quality and go for unbreakable, airtight containers that are easy to wash up.

Bottles

Next, you will need bottles to store broths, stocks, juices etc. Try to buy bottles that are hardy and long lasting. You can buy whatever quantity you need depending on how much you think will be prepare in advance. The bottles should fit in the fridge or freezer. They should be BPA free and also free from odor.

Cling film

You will require cling film to cover some of the bowls or boxes containing the prepped ingredients. Buy good quality cling film that can serve multiple purposes. Have 2 or 3 spare rolls that are easily available whenever you need them.

Aluminum foil

You will need aluminum foil to cover or wrap the prepped ingredients. This is especially important if you want something to remain warm. Using foil can also ensure tenderizing of meats and vegetables. Buy good quality foil and have 2 or 3 spare rolls in stock.

Ziploc bags

Ziploc bags are a must when you wish to prep for a meal. Ziploc bags not only seal in moisture and flavor but also prevent the foods from going bad. They are also easy to store in the fridge or freezer and take up far less space when compared to containers.

Now that you know what you need to buy in order to store the prepped ingredients, we will look at how you can prep some of the different elements of a meal.

Vegetables and fruits

It is extremely important for you to prep your vegetables and fruits well in advance. Vegetables are extremely important for your body. You have to consume at least 5 different types of vegetables on a daily basis. The best way to prep is by washing them thoroughly before peeling and chopping. Once done, transfer them to containers that are clean and dry. The same extends to fruits. You must wash and chop them before adding to containers. If you do not wish to chop the vegetables or fruits just before cooking, then you can wash, peel and add them to Ziploc bags. Store the bags in the freezer if you wish to use them much later or in the fridge, if you plan on using them very soon.

Meats

Meats are one of the most important parts of a meal. They are rich in protein and can help build leaner muscles. There are many types of meats to choose from and you can pick whatever you are comfortable with. The best way to prep meats is by first cleaning them thoroughly by rinsing them. You must try to get rid of as many germs from the meat as possible. Once done, chop it to the desired size and add to the containers. If you wish to marinate the meats, then first prepare the marinade and add to the container before adding in the meat. It will be best to pick containers for wet marinades and Ziploc bags for dry rubs.

Carbohydrates

Carbohydrates are generally regarded as villains considering the effect they can have on the body. However, not all carbs are bad carbs and it is essential for your body to eat a minimum amount in order to carry out basic activities. There are many sources of carbohydrates but is best to choose whole grains such as quinoa, wheat, barley etc. Switching up white rice with brown rice can also help you tackle some of the issues associated with carbohydrate intake. To prep carbs, you have to ensure that everything is dry as even a little moisture can end up spoiling your ingredients. If you are mixing them with vegetables then try to dry the vegetables before adding in the carbs.

Liquids

When it comes to storing liquids, you have to choose airtight bottles that are sturdy and spill proof. You can store many types of liquids including stocks, sauces, broths, soups, stews etc. Bone broth is a great liquid to have in your pantry, as it is full of healthy nutrients. It is also quite versatile and can be added to prepare a variety of meals. You can easily prepare the broth at home by adding bones and water to a cooker and setting it on manual for 40 minutes. Wait for it to cool down before discarding the bones and straining the liquid into bottles.

Sides

No meal is complete without sides and so you must prep for them in order to have a complete meal. Right from pickles to relishes, you can prepare sides in advance and store them in airtight containers. Place them in the fridge if you use them on a daily basis. If you wish to store a large batch then add it to the freezer.

Snacks

You can prep and store snacks the same way as you would regular meals. You can store chopped vegetables such as carrots, beetroots, celery sticks etc. and add them to airtight containers. You can also pack dips to go along with them.

Meals

If you wish to store entire meals in containers then it will take a lot more effort from your end, but is well worth it considering you won't have to cook after a busy day. Here are some pointers to help you out

If you plan on storing food for a week then ensure that it contains ingredients that can last that long. You can refer to a chart that tells you what foods can be stored for a week without spoiling.

If you wish to store cooked meals in the fridge then ensure you consume them within 3 days. You have to add them to the freezer if you plan on consuming them after 3 days.

Always check the food by first smelling it. If it does not smell good, then discard it. Some foods can smell good but taste bad so eat a small quantity first to determine whether the meal is good enough to be consumed.

Try to label your foods with dates so that you know when the food was prepared.

Do not put a used spoon or fork into the food and then store it. This will spoil the food. The same extends to using your fingers.

Saves money – There is a prevalent view that adhering to a good diet propensities are excessively costly. In any case, that isn't really right. Do you go to the store each day to purchase something to cook? Despite everything you don't comprehend what to get ready, so you purchase a bundle of unfortunate things. This must be hurtful for your financial plan. Supper preparing permits you to spare cash since arranging dinners keeps you from heading off to the store each day. Besides, looking for this practice requires acquiring things in mass, which is less expensive. In case you're on a tight spending plan, or basically need to spare cash for something else, e.g. excursion, then dinner arranging is the ideal answer for you.

Easier shopping – Dinner preparing permits you to remain composed with regards to looking for basic needs. You simply need to recognize what to cook, prepare, and look for fixings. With a solitary outing to the grocery store, you can get all that will requirement for that week or even a month.

More variety – Individuals will probably eat similar dinners again and again without the feast arrange. The reason is straightforward: you like the feast, it's anything but difficult to get ready, and you make it at whatever point you can. Yet, your body needs greater differences, as various nutrition classes convey distinctive supplements to your life form. While preparing dinners, you get the opportunity to bring assortment into your dietary patterns.

Multitask – Is it true that you are a bustling individual with a feverish calendar? Feast preparing is perfect for you, and in case you're going to inquire as to why then you ought to endure as the main priority that it will permit you to invest less energy in the kitchen. This permits you to show signs of improvement and fulfill more things on the double.

More energy, less effort – When you prepare, you should simply open the cooler, get a feast of your decision, and reestablish your vitality levels. This will likewise support your efficiency.

Breakfast

Zucchini Apple Oat Waffles

- Prep Time: 15 minutes
- Cook Time: 2-3 minutes per waffle
- Serving Size: 114 g
- Serves: 4
- Calories: 242

Ingredients:

- 3 eggs
- 2 teaspoons baking powder
- 1/2 teaspoon salt
- 1/2 teaspoon nutmeg
- 1/2 teaspoon baking soda
- 1/2 cup zucchini, shredded
- 1/2 cup apple, shredded
- 1 teaspoon cinnamon
- 1 cup oats, old-fashioned
- 1 1/2 cups low-fat buttermilk
- 1 1/2 cups almond flour
- 4 tablespoons butter, melted

Directions:

1. Inside a large-sized bowl, whisk the oats with the flour, baking soda, baking powder, cinnamon, salt, and nutmeg.

2. Add the buttermilk, eggs, and melted butter; whisk until the mixture is well combined. Stir in the apple and the zucchini.

3. Cook the batter in a Belgian waffle maker until golden and crisp. Serve immediately with butter and maple syrup or honey, or with a poached egg. I love to serve mine with honey and freshly sliced apples.

4. Notes: The batter can be made a night before; just store in the fridge. You can also freeze a batch. When ready to serve, just heat in the toaster.

Crispy Sweet Potato Waffles

- Prep Time: 20 minutes
- Cook Time: 10 minutes
- Serving Size: 166 g
- Serves: 4
- Calories: 366

Ingredients:

- 1 cup sweet potato puree
- 1 egg
- 1 teaspoon salt
- 1/3 cup cornmeal
- 1/4 cup oil
- 2 teaspoons baking powder
- 3/4 cup almond flour
- 3/4 cup milk

Directions:

1. Steam the sweet potato cubes for about 10 minutes or till soft; using a hand mixer, blend or mash until smooth.
2. Combine the sweet potato puree with the egg, milk, and oil; mix until well combined.

3. In another bowl, combine the flour with the baking powder, cornmeal, and salt. Add the wet ingredients into the dry ingredients; mix until just combined.

4. Cook the batter into a greased waffle maker for about 3 to 4 minutes or till cooked through. Serve immediately or, if not serving right away, let cool completely.

Breakfast Eggs and Bacon Burritos

- Prep Time: 5 minutes
- Cook Time: 10 minutes
- Serving Size: 176 g
- Serves: 4
- Calories: 279

Ingredients:

- 8 eggs, large
- 4 piece bacon, thick-cut, cooked until crispy
- 4 Multi-Grain with Flax flatbreads
- 1 tablespoon garlic, minced
- 1 tablespoon extra-virgin olive oil
- 1 red pepper, finely minced
- 1/2 red onion, finely minced
- Salt and pepper, to taste
- Splash milk

Directions:

1. Put the olive oil and the minced garlic into a medium-sized saucepan. Turn the heat to medium-high; cook until the oil is heated.
2. Inside a large-sized bowl, whisk the eggs with a splash of milk; set aside.
3. Add the onion and the red pepper into the saucepan; sauté for a couple of minutes or till the onions start to become translucent.
4. Add the egg mix to the saucepan; sauté for about 3 to 5 minutes or till cooked.
5. Put 1/4 of the egg mix and 1 piece of cooked bacon on top of the bread. Sprinkle with cheese. Wrap tightly and enjoy.

Walnut Apricot Bars

- Prep Time: 15 minutes
- Cook Time: 0 minutes
- Serving Size: 51 g
- Serves: 6
- Calories: 171

Ingredients:

- 1 cup walnuts
- 1 lemon, zested
- 1 tablespoon chia seeds
- 1 tablespoon hemp seeds
- 1 tablespoon lemon juice
- 1/2 cup dried apricot
- 1/4 cup goji berries

- 4 dates, pits removed, soak in water for 10 mins

Directions:

1. Soak the dates in warm water for about 10 minutes or till softened a bit; drain the water.
2. Put all the ingredients into a food processor; process until almost smooth, but not completely.
3. Pour the mixture into a baking tray; freeze for about 10-15 minutes or until set.
4. Cut into bars and store in the fridge.

Apple Pecan Hemp Hearts Granola

- Prep Time: 5 minutes
- Cook Time: 35 minutes
- Serving Size: 72 g
- Serves: 10
- Calories: 284

Ingredients:

- 3 cups rolled oats (gluten-free if necessary)
- 1/4 cup coconut oil, melted
- 1/3 cup sugar-free maple syrup
- 1/2 cup unsweetened dried apple rings, chopped
- 1/2 cup unsweetened applesauce
- 1/2 cup hemp seeds
- 1 teaspoon vanilla extract
- 1 teaspoon cinnamon
- 1 1/2 cups pecans, chopped
- 1 egg white, whipped, optional

Directions:

1. Preheat the oven to 350F.

2. Inside a large-sized bowl, combine the oats with the hemp hearts, pecans, and cinnamon.

3. Add the applesauce, coconut oil, vanilla extract, honey, and egg white; stir until the well combined and the oat is well coated.

4. Line a baking sheet with a silicone mat or parchment paper. Spread the granola onto the baking sheet; bake for 15 minutes.

5. Remove the baking sheet from the oven. Flip the granola as well as you can. Return the baking sheet to the oven; bake for 15 to 20 minutes more.

6. Remove the baking sheet from the oven; let the granola cool completely on the baking sheet. When cool, add the dried apple rings.

Baked Almond Dark Chocolate Oatmeal

- Prep Time: 10 minutes
- Cook Time: 35 minutes
- Serving Size: 139 g
- Serves: 6
- Calories: 241

Ingredients:

- 1 1/2 ounces dark chocolate, 70%,
- 1 1/2 tablespoons coconut oil,
- 1 3/4 cup almond milk
- 1 3/4 cups rolled oats
- 1 large egg
- 1 teaspoon baking powder
- 1 teaspoon cinnamon
- 1/2 cup ripe banana, mashed
- 1/2 cup salted almonds, chopped
- 1/4 teaspoon almond extract
- 2 teaspoons vanilla extract
- Sea salt, for sprinkling on top

For sprinkling on top:

- Chopped salted almonds
- Banana slices

Directions:

1. Preheat the oven to 350F. Grease a 9-inch baking dish and 9-inch skillet with non-stick cooking spray or oil.
2. Inside a large-sized bowl, whisk the oats with the baking powder, chopped almonds, and the cinnamon.
3. In another bowl, mix the mashed banana with the egg, almond milk, coconut oil, almond extract, and vanilla until well combined.
4. Add the wet ingredients into the dry ingredients; mix to combine. Pour the mix into the prepared dish or skillet; smooth the top. Sprinkle the

4. Chocolate chunks or chips over the top; bake for about 32 to 37 minutes or till the edges start to turn slightly golden brown. If desired, top with bananas, sprinkle with sea salt, and chopped almonds before baking. Serve warm with almond milk.

Sausage and Kale Waffle Stratta

Ingredients:

- 1 pound breakfast sausage, ground, pork, turkey
- 8 large eggs
- 6 almond flour waffles, toasted
- 3 cups kale, stems removed, roughly chopped
- 1/4 cup unsweetened almond milk, non-dairy
- 1 tablespoon olive oil for greasing the pan
- Cheese, crumbled or grated, optional
- Red pepper flakes, optional
- Sea salt and pepper, to taste

Directions:

1. Preheat the oven to 350F if baking right away. Lightly grease an 8x8-inch glass baking pan or a casserole dish with olive oil or butter or your choice.

2. Heat a skillet over medium-high heat. Add the ground sausage; cook until lightly browned. Remove from the skillet and then set aside. Add the kale in the same skillet; quickly wilt; remove from the skillet and

set aside. In a bowl, whisk the eggs with the milk and a season of salt and pepper to taste; set aside.

3. Dice the toasted waffles into 1-2 inch square pieces. Layer 1/2 of the waffle squared into the bottom of the prepared pan. Add 1/2 of the browned sausage and then 1/2 of the wilted kale. If using cheese, sprinkle 1/2 of the cheese over the top.

4. Layer the remaining waffle squares, sausage, and the kale. Pour the egg mix over the top. Sprinkle with the remaining cheese, if using, and season with salt and pepper to taste. Sprinkle with the red pepper flakes, if desired. If desired, let the mixture sit overnight to allow the waffles to absorb the egg mix. But you can bake right away.

5. Bake for about 45 minutes to 1 hour or until the eggs are set and the strata are firm and a knife comes out clean when inserted in the middle. Bake for 5 to 10 minutes more, if needed. When baked, let sit for 10 minutes before cutting or scooping into portions.

Savory Sweet Potato, Turkey and Egg Bowl

Ingredients:

- 1 avocado, sliced
- 1 cup red onion, chopped
- 2 cups sweet potatoes, cooked, cubed
- 2 red pepper, chopped
- 4 eggs
- 4 tablespoons hot sauce, optional
- 8 cups greens
- 8 ounces turkey sausage, nitrate-free
- 8 tablespoons coconut oil or extra virgin olive oil
- Salt and pepper, to taste

Directions:

1. Heat 1 tablespoon of coconut or extra-virgin olive oil in a medium - large sized pan on the stove. Add the sweet potato cubes; sauté for about 10 minutes or till the edges start to golden. Remove from the pan and set aside.

2. In the same pan, add the turkey sausages and cook until brown. Remove from the pan and set aside.

3. In the same pan, add the onion, red pepper, and the greens; sauté for 3 minutes.

4. In a different pan, fry about 1-2 eggs with 1 tablespoon of oil until over easy or until cooked to your desired doneness.

5. Divide the veggies, greens, sweet potato cubes, and turkey sausages between 4 bowls. Top each serves with the fried eggs. Season with salt and pepper and, if desired, serve with hot sauce.

Breakfast Harvest Cookies

Ingredients:

- 1 cup banana, mashed
- 1 teaspoon baking soda
- 1/2 cup pumpkin puree
- 1/2 cup raisins
- 1/2 cup unsweetened coconut, shredded
- 1/3 cup coconut flour
- 1/4 teaspoon ginger
- 2 teaspoons apple cider vinegar
- 2 teaspoons cinnamon
- 4 dates, soft

Directions:

1. Preheat the oven to 350F. Line a baking sheet with parchment paper or Silpat.
2. Put the mashed banana, dates, and the pumpkin puree in a blender or a food processor; blend or process until the dates are mixed well with the purees. Add the flour, baking soda, ginger, cinnamon, and vinegar; blend or process again until the mixture is a thick batter.
3. Gently fold in the raisins and the shredded coconut. By heaping tablespoons, scoop the batter onto the prepared baking sheet. With

your hands, flatten them into cookie shapes. Bake for about 20-25 minutes

4. Or until the center of the cookies are not too soft to touch and the edges are golden. Let them cool in pan for about 15 minutes on the baking sheet since they will turn very soft when baked.

5. With a spatula, transfer then to wire racks and let cool completely. Serve immediately or store in the fridge for up to 7 days.

Nutty Fruity Baked Oatmeal

Ingredients:

- 2 cups oats, old-fashioned
- 1/4 cup nuts, chopped walnuts or almonds
- 1/3 cup dried fruit (raisins, cranberries, and cherries)
- 1/2 cup unsweetened applesauce
- 1/2 cup packed brown sugar
- 1 teaspoon baking powder
- 1 large egg
- 1 1/2 cups 2% milk
- 2 tablespoons butter, melted

Directions:

1. Preheat the oven to 375F.
2. Stir the oats with the brown sugar, dried fruits, nuts, and the baking powder in a bowl.
3. In another bowl, whisk the milk with the egg, butter, and applesauce. Stir the milk mix into the oat mixture until well combined.
4. Grease a 7x11-inch baking dish with nonstick spray. Pour the batter into the dish; level the top and then bake for 20 minutes.
5. When baked, let cool and then cut into serving portions.

Breakfast Burritos

Ingredients:

- 1 pound turkey sausage
- 1 green or red sweet pepper, chopped
- 1 small onion, chopped
- 1 tablespoon olive oil
- 1/2 teaspoon pepper
- 1/2 teaspoon salt
- 12 large eggs
- 1-2 tablespoon cheese per serving, shredded
- 12-14 tortillas, medium-sized
- 1/2 cup 2% milk, optional
- Salsa, optional

Directions:

1. Line a baking sheet with wax paper.
2. Heat the olive oil in a large-sized skillet on medium heat. Add the turkey, onion, and pepper; cook, breaking the sausage into tiny pieces and sauté until completely cooked and browned. Set aside.
3. Inside a large-sized bowl, whisk the eggs with the milk and seasoning of the salt and pepper until combined.

4. Over medium heat, heat a large-sized nonstick frying pan. Add 1 tablespoon of butter and let melt. When the butter is melted, add the eggs; scramble until cooked.

5. Warm the tortilla in the microwave according to directions on the package.

6. Layer 1/2 cup of scrambled eggs, 1/2 cup of sausage mix, about 1 to 2 tablespoon of cheese, and a bit of salsa on a warm tortilla; fold into a burrito.

Cheesy Bacon and Eggs Oat Muffins

Ingredients:

- 6 large eggs
- 1 cup almond flour
- 1/4 cup Canadian bacon, chopped
- 1/3 cup oats, old-fashioned
- 1/2 teaspoon salt
- 1/2 cup red pepper, chopped
- 1/2 cup cheddar cheese, shredded
- 1 tablespoon baking powder
- 1/4 cup fresh parsley, chopped
- 1/4 cup unsweetened applesauce
- 1/4 teaspoon cinnamon
- 1/4 teaspoon pepper

Directions:

1. Preheat the oven to 375F.Inside a large-sized bowl, whisk the eggs with the applesauce until well combined.

2. In a different bowl, combine the flour with the baking powder, oats, cinnamon, and season with salt and pepper. Add the flour mix into the egg mix; stir till just combined. Mix in the cheese, the bacon, parsley, and the pepper.

3. Grease a 12-muffin pan with nonstick spray. Pour the batter into the muffin cups and bake for about 15-20 minutes or till baked through; The muffin tops should be set and a toothpick should come out clean when inserted in the muffin. Put the muffin pan on a wire rack and let cool for 5 minutes. Remove from the muffin cups and let cool completely on the wire rack.

Maple, Pecan, and Sour Cherry Granola Bars

Ingredients:

- 2 cups oats, old-fashioned
- 1/3 cup light brown sugar
- 1/2 teaspoon kosher salt
- 1/2 cup wheat germ
- 1/2 cup golden flaxseed
- 1/2 cup almonds, sliced
- 1 large egg white, beaten
- 1 cup unsweetened coconut shavings
- 1 cup pumpkin seeds (pepitas)
- 1 cup pecans, chopped
- 1 cup dried sour cherries
- 1 1/2 teaspoons vanilla extract
- 3 tablespoons virgin coconut oil
- 3/4 cup sugar-free maple syrup

Directions:

1. Preheat the oven to 375F. On a rimmed baking sheet, toss the oats with the pecans, coconut, pumpkin seeds, almonds, and flax seeds. Toast in the oven, occasionally stirring, for about 10 to 15 minutes or till slightly golden.

2. Reduce the temperature of the oven to 325F; transfer the mix into a large-sized bowl, stir in the cherries and the wheat germ. Mix the maple syrup with the coconut oil, brown sugar substitute, salt, and vanilla in a small-sized saucepan; bring to a boil and cook for about 4 minutes, occasionally stirring, until the sugar is dissolved. Let cool for 15 minutes and then whisk the egg white in.

3. Pour the maple syrup mix over the oat mix; stir until well coated.

4. Line a different baking sheet with rim with parchment paper. Scrape the oat mix and bake for about 45 to 55 minutes or till deep golden brown. Let cool for 30 minutes and then cut into bars. Notes: Make these bars ahead of time and store in airtight containers for up to 3 weeks.

Toasted Coconut Pumpkin Bread

Ingredients:

- 1 1/4 cups all-purpose flour
- 1 cup (packed) light brown sugar
- 1 cup pure pumpkin, canned
- 1 tablespoon granulated sugar
- 1 teaspoon ground cinnamon
- 1 teaspoon ground ginger
- 1 teaspoon kosher salt
- 1/2 cup virgin coconut oil, slightly cooled
- 1/2 cup whole-wheat flour
- 1/4 teaspoon ground allspice
- 1/4 teaspoon ground nutmeg
- 1/8 teaspoon ground cloves
- 2 large eggs, room temperature
- 2 tablespoons raw pumpkin seeds (pepitas)
- 2 tablespoons unsweetened coconut flakes
- 2 teaspoons baking powder
- Nonstick vegetable oil spray

Directions:

1. Preheat the oven to 350F. Lightly grease a 4 1/2 x 8 1/2 loaf pan with nonstick spray and then line with parchment paper, leaving a 2-inch overhang on all sides.

2. Whisk the all-purpose flour with the wheat flour, the baking powder, ginger, cinnamon, allspice, salt, nutmeg, and cloves inside a large sized bowl.

3. Whisk the eggs with the brown sugar substitute, pumpkin, and oil in another large-sized bowl until smooth.

4. Mix the wet ingredients into the dry ingredients mix. Scrape the batter into the prepared pan, smooth the top, and then sprinkle with the coconut, pumpkin seeds, and the granulated sugar substitute.

4. Bake the bread for about 50 to 60 minutes or till golden brown or a toothpick comes out clean when inserted in the center.

5. Transfer the pan to a wire rack and let cool in pan for 30 minutes. Turn the bread out onto the wire rack; let cool completely.

Cashew, Sesame, and Flaxseed Bars

Ingredients:

- 6 tablespoons raw sesame seeds
- 5 tablespoons flaxseed
- 3/4 teaspoon kosher salt
- 1/4 teaspoon ground cardamom
- 1/4 cup wheat bran
- 1/2 cup pure maple syrup
- 1 tablespoon coconut oil
- 1 1/2 cups cashews
- Nonstick vegetable oil spray

Directions:

1. Preheat the oven to 350F. Grease an 8x8 baking pan with vegetable oil spray and then line with parchment paper, leaving an overhang on all the sides.

2. In another rimmed baking sheet, put the cashews, flaxseed, and the sesame seeds without mixing them; toast in the oven, occasionally stirring, but not mixing, for about 10-12 minutes or till golden brown. Let cool; set aside 1 tablespoon of flaxseed and 2 tablespoons of sesame seeds.

3. Process the cashews and the remaining seeds with the wheat bran, cinnamon, and salt in a food processor until the mix is mostly finely chopped; transfer to a medium-sized bowl.

4. Mix the maple syrup with the coconut oil in a small-sized saucepan; bring to a boil, stirring, for 1 minute. Pour in the cashew mix; stir until well coated.

5. Wet hands and firmly press the mix into the prepared pan. Top with the reserved 1 tablespoon of flaxseed and 2 tablespoons of sesame seeds; press to adhere. Bake for about 25 to 30 minutes or until golden brown; let cool and then cut into bars.

Cherry-Almond Granola Bars

Ingredients:

- 3/4 cup unsweetened coconut, finely shredded
- 3/4 cup raw almonds, whole
- 3/4 cup dried tart cherries, coarsely chopped
- 2 tablespoons flaxseeds, toasted
- 2 1/4 cups oats, old-fashioned
- 1/4 cup coconut oil, plus more
- 1/2 cup sunflower seeds, unsalted, roasted
- 1/2 cup honey
- 1/2 cup (packed) light brown sugar
- 1 teaspoon kosher salt

Directions:

1. Preheat the oven to 400F.
2. Ina large-sized, heavy rimmed baking sheet, mix the oats with the almonds; bake for about 10 minutes, stirring once, until just golden. Transfer the baking sheet on a wire rack and let cool on the baking sheet.
3. Reduce the temperature of the oven to 325F.

4. Meanwhile, brush a 9x13x2-inch glass or metal baking dish with coconut oil and then line with parchment paper, leaving a generous overhang on the long sides. Brush the parchment paper with oil.

5. Generously brush a large-sized bowl with oil. Put the oat mix, coconut, cherries, flaxseeds, and sunflower seeds into the bowl.

6. Mix 1/4 cup of oil with the light brown sugar substitute, salt, and honey in a medium-sized, heavy, deep saucepan; bring to a boil; boil for 1 minute, stirring to dissolve the sugar.

7. Transfer the pan to a wire rack; let the granola cool completely in pan. Hold the paper overhang and lift the granola from the pan. Cut into 24 bars.

Better Oat Granola with Coconut and Sesame Seeds

Ingredients:

- 3 cups oats, old-fashioned
- 2 tablespoons (packed) light brown sugar
- 1/4 cup sesame seeds
- 1/4 cup olive oil or warmed coconut oil
- 1/2 teaspoon ground cinnamon
- 1/2 cup agave syrup
- 1 large egg white, lightly beaten
- 1 cup dried cherries or cranberries
- 1 1/2 teaspoons kosher salt
- 1 1/2 cups nuts, chopped
- 1 1/2 cups coconut shavings

Directions:

1. Preheat the oven to 300F.
2. Inside a large-sized bowl, toss the egg whites with the oats, coconut shavings, nuts, oil, agave syrup, brown sugar substitute, sesame seeds, cinnamon, and salt. Spread the mix on a rimmed baking sheet; bake for about 40 to 45 minutes, stirring every 10 minutes, until golden

3. Brown. When baked, let cool on the baking sheet. The mix will become crispier as it cools. Mix in the cherries.

4. Serve over low-fat yogurt or layer in a glass with yogurt and fresh fruits.

Pistachio-Prune Oat Bars

Ingredients:

- 1 1/2 cups oats, old-fashioned
- 1 cup dried figs, chopped
- 1 cup prunes, chopped
- 1 tablespoon orange juice, fresh
- 1/2 teaspoon orange zest, finely grated
- 1/2 vanilla bean, split lengthwise
- 2 tablespoons coconut oil
- 3 tablespoons plus 1 cup pistachios
- 3/4teaspoon kosher salt
- Nonstick vegetable oil spray

Directions:

1. Preheat the oven to 200F. Lightly grease an 8x8-inch baking pan with vegetable oil spray and then line with parchment paper, leaving a generous overhang on all sides.

2. Inside a large-sized skillet, heat the coconut oil on medium heat. Add the oats, cook, stirring frequently, for about 4 minutes or until golden brown. Transfer to a plate and let cool.

3. Meanwhile, put 3 tablespoons of pistachios into a food processor, process until finely ground and then transfer into a small-sized bowl.

4. Scrape the vanilla bean seeds into the food processor. Add the prunes, figs, 1/2 cup of pistachios, orange juice, orange zest, and 2 tablespoons

5. Of water; process until smooth. Transfer the mix into a medium-sized bowl.

6. Coarsely chop the remaining 1/2 cup of pistachios; add into the medium-sized bowl. Add the oats; mix well. Firmly press the mix into the prepared baking pan and then sprinkle with the ground pistachios, pressing to adhere. Bake for about 20-25 minutes or till no longer sticky; let cool and then cut into bars.

Cheesy Carrot, Corn, and Peas Muffins

Ingredients:

- 1 1/2 cups carrots, shredded (about 4 carrots)
- 1/2 cup frozen corn
- 1/2 cup frozen peas
- 1/2 cup orange bell peppers, small diced
- 12 tablespoons mozzarella cheese, shredded
- 8 large eggs
- Salt and pepper, to taste

Directions:

1. Preheat the oven to 375F. Generously grease a nonstick 12-cup regular-sized muffin pan with cooking spray. Spray the sides and the base; run your finger over the sides to liberally coat. Make sure the muffin cups are generously coated with oil or you chisel off stuck food. Set aside.

2. Inside a large-sized bowl, toss the carrots with the peas, corn, peppers until combined. You can mix and match your favorite veggies.

3. Loosely pile about 3 tablespoons of the veggie mix into each muffin cup; fill each cup about 2/3-3/4 full, evenly distributing the filling the mix between the cups until all the filling is gone. Set the pan aside.

4. In a 2-cup glass measuring cup, crack the eggs lightly beat using a whisk. The measuring cup will make pouring easier. Season the egg with salt and pepper to taste and whisk to combine. Pour about 2 to 3 tablespoons of the egg mix into each cup, distributing evenly. The cups will be 3/4 full.

5. Top each cup with a generous pinch of cheese, about 1 tablespoon each; bake for about 18 to 20 minutes or till the muffins are set, cooked through, and lightly golden.

6. The muffins will puff in the oven, but they sink when cooling. Transfer the muffin pan onto a wire rack; let the muffins cool in the muffin pan for about 10 minutes. Run a knife around the edges of the muffin and then with a small spoon, pop the muffins out from the muffin pan.

Vegetarian Make-Ahead Freezer Breakfast Sandwiches

Ingredients:

- 12 eggs
- 12 sausage patties
- 12 whole-wheat English muffins
- 3/4 cup cheddar cheese, shredded

Directions:

1. Preheat the oven to 350F. Grease a regular muffin tin with nonstick cooking spray or coat with coconut oil.

2. Crack 1 egg into each muffin cup; bake for about 20-25 minutes or till the eggs are set. Let the eggs cool to room temperature; this will prevent the English muffins from becoming soggy.

3. Slice the English muffins into bottom and top halves. Place 1 sausage patty onto each muffin bottom halves, sprinkle with a pinch of cheese, top with egg, and then with the muffin tops.

Gluten-Free Carrot Cake Breakfast Cookies

Ingredients:

- 2 cups oats, old fashioned, gluten-free certified
- 1/4 cup honey
- 1/4 cup ground flaxseed meal, gluten-free
- 1/4 cup coconut oil, melted
- 1/4 cup almond milk (or any kind)
- 1/2 teaspoons salt
- 1/2 teaspoon baking soda
- 1/2 cup unsweetened applesauce
- 1/2 cup pecans, gluten-free, finely chopped
- 1/2 cup banana, very ripe, mashed
- 1 teaspoon cinnamon
- 1 cup carrots, finely grated
- 1 1/4 cups oat flour
- 2 tablespoons maple syrup

Directions:

1. Preheat the oven to 350F. Line a baking sheet with parchment paper or Silpat; set aside.

2. Inside a large-sized bowl, mix the oats with the flaxseed meal, oat flour, baking soda, cinnamon, and salt until combined.

3. In another bowl, mix the mashed bananas with the honey, applesauce, milk, coconut oil, and maple syrup until combined. Add the wet ingredients into the dry ingredients; mix. Add the grated carrots and the chopped pecans; mix until combined.

4. With an ice cream scooper, scoop about 1/4 cup worth of batter into the prepared baking sheet. Wet hands with water and then press the batter down to flatten slightly into cookies. Bake for about 8-10 minutes or until golden brown.

Ham and Cheese Waffle Sandwiches

Ingredients:

- 8 waffles
- 4 1/2 ounces deli ham, sliced
- 4 slices cheddar cheese, sharp, sliced

Directions:

1. Top each 4 waffles with 1 slice of cheese and 2 slices of ham. Top each with the remaining waffles, making waffle sandwiches.

2. Place the waffle sandwiches into a baking sheet; broil for about 4 to 5 minutes or till the cheese is melted and the outside is crispy.

Lunch

Bacon & Asparagus Quiche
Makes: 6-8 servings

Ingredients

- ½ tbsp. butter
- ½ cup bacon (Diced, cooked)
- ½ tbsp. olive oil
- 2 ¾ cups asparagus (Diced, cooked)
- 1/3 cup onion (Diced)
- 1 tsp mixed herbs
- 1 ¼ cups mushrooms (Sliced)
- ½ tsp salt
- 1 cup ricotta cheese
- ½ tsp pepper
- 1 cup plain yogurt
- ½ tsp nutmeg
- 4 eggs

Directions:

1. Preheat your oven to 400 Fahrenheit. Grease a pie pan with butter, and set to one side.
2. Now heat the mushrooms, olive oil and onions in a skillet, and sauté on a medium heat, until the onions are clear.

3. Set to one side. Take a bowl, and add the eggs, cheese, and yogurt, and stir until the mix is nice and creamy.
4. Add the salt, pepper, herbs, and nutmeg, and stir again. Now take the bacon, mushroom mix and asparagus, and fold it gently into the cheese mix.
5. Spoon this mixture into your pie pan, and place in the oven.
6. Cook for 35-40 minutes, or until the eggs are springy, and the quiche is going a little brown around the edges.
7. Allow to cool, and cut into portions.

Grilled Chicken & Roasted Vegetables
Makes: 8 servings

Ingredients

- 2 cups quinoa (Cooked)
- 2 lbs. boneless skinless chicken breasts
- 2 cups rice (Cooked)
- 4 cups cauliflower florets
- 4 cups asparagus
- 2 tbsp. taco seasoning
- 1 tbsp. garlic powder
- 1 tbsp. onion powder
- Olive oil
- Salt and pepper

Directions:

1. Preheat oven to 400 degrees Fahrenheit. Spray two baking sheets with nonstick cooking spray.
2. Toss the cauliflower and asparagus with a bit of olive oil and sprinkle with salt and pepper, garlic powder and onion powder.
3. Place evenly on one of the baking sheets. On the other sheet place chicken breasts.
4. Drizzle olive oil and then sprinkle with taco seasoning or seasoning of your choice.
5. Place both sheets into preheated oven and cook for 20-25 minutes flipping halfway.
6. Once cooked, cube the chicken. Place the rice, quinoa, cauliflower and asparagus into a bowl, and mix well.
7. Add the chicken on top, and mix a little.
8. Divide into 8 portions.

Tuna Salad Sandwich
Makes: 4 servings

Ingredients

- 10 ounces tuna in water
- 4 sandwich thins
- ¼ cup plain yogurt
- 4 slices provolone cheese

- ½ tsp lemon juice
- ½ tsp honey
- ½ cup carrot (Grated)
- ¼ tsp garlic powder
- ¼ tsp dill
- ¼ cup red onion (Diced)
- ¼ tsp Dijon mustard
- ½ tsp parsley (Chopped)
- ¼ tsp salt

Directions:

1. Add all the ingredients apart from the Provolone, and the sandwich things to a bowl.
2. Mix well, and then spread the mixture into the sandwich things.
3. Sprinkle the cheese on top.

Slow Cooker Lo Mein
Makes: 6 servings

Ingredients

- 2 lbs. boneless pork shoulder
- 3 cups broccoli florets
- 2 carrots, julienned

- 2 stalks celery, diced
- 1 cup snow peas
- 1 can of water chestnuts, drained
- 1 pound of noodles of your choice

Sauce:

- 1/3 cup reduced sodium soy sauce
- 3 cloves garlic, minced
- 2 tbsp. brown sugar
- 1 tbsp. sambal oelek
- 1 tbsp. oyster sauce
- 1 tbsp. grated ginger
- 1 tsp sesame oil

Directions:

1. Whisk together soy sauce, garlic, brown sugar, sambal oelek, oyster sauce, and ginger and sesame oil in the slow cooker.
2. Add pork shoulder and cover and cook on low for 7-8 hours.
3. Remove pork shoulder and shred the meat then return to the slow cooker. Add in the broccoli, carrots, celery, snow peas and chestnuts.
4. Cook on high for 15-30 minutes or until veggies are tender. Cook noodles according to their package.
5. Serve noodles topped with pork and veggies.
6. Separate into containers for easy heat up meals for the week!

Italian-style Chicken and Tomato Soup

Makes: 6 servings

Ingredients

- 3 chicken breasts (Boneless, skinless)
- Pepper
- 1 onion (Chopped)
- ½ tsp salt
- 2 garlic cloves (Minced)
- 1 tbsp. basil
- 1 can coconut milk
- 2 tbsp. Italian seasoning
- 1 cup chicken broth
- 14 ounces diced tomatoes

Directions:

1. Add all the ingredients apart from the chicken to your slow cooker.
2. Stir well, and then add your chicken.
3. Cook on a high heat for 4-6 hours, or until the chicken is easy to shred.
4. Take the chicken out of the slow cooker, shred it using two forks, then add it back in and stir well.

Greek Chicken Bowls
Makes: 8 servings

Ingredients

Chicken:

- 2 lbs. boneless skinless chicken breasts
- ¼ cup olive oil
- 1 tbsp. red wine vinegar
- 1 tbsp. dried oregano
- 3 tbsp. minced garlic
- 1/3 cup fresh lemon juice
- 1/3 cup plain Greek yogurt
- Salt and pepper to taste

Cucumber Salad:

- 2 English cucumbers peeled and sliced
- 1/3 cup lemon juice
- 2 tbsp. olive oil
- 1 tbsp. minced garlic
- ½ tsp dried oregano

Tzatziki Sauce:

- 1 cup plain Greek Yogurt
- 1 English cucumber finely diced

- 1 tbsp. minced garlic
- ½ tbsp. dill weed
- 1 tbsp. fresh lemon juice
- 1 tsp lemon zest
- ½ tsp chopped fresh mint (optional)
- Salt and pepper to taste

Other stuff:

- 3 cups cooked brown rice
- 1 ½ pounds cherry tomatoes cut in half
- ½ cup red onion slices

Directions:

1. In a large plastic bag combine olive oil, garlic, lemon juice, red wine vinegar, oregano, Greek yogurt and salt and pepper.
2. Massage to mix. Add chicken into bag and massage to fully cover chicken then let marinate for at least 20 minutes (up to 12 hours).
3. Drain the chicken and discard the remainder of marinade. In a skillet heat some oil over medium heat and add chicken once hot.
4. Flip halfway through cooking (approx. 3-4 minutes per side depending on size of chicken) Remove from pan and let cool.
5. Cut into bite size pieces. To make cucumber salad cut up cucumbers into chunks and toss in a bowl with the lemon juice, olive oil, red wine vinegar, garlic, and oregano. Set aside.
6. For the tzatziki sauce combine the Greek yogurt, cucumber, garlic dill, lemon juice and zest, and season with salt and pepper.

7. Cook brown rice and divide into meal prep containers (1/2 cup per container), add in cherry tomatoes and mix with red onions in each bowl.
8. Top each bowl with chicken, cucumber salad and some tzatziki sauce.
9. Serve cold!

Zucchini and Lemon Risotto
Makes: 2 servings

Ingredients

- ½ cup butter
- 2 tbsp. crème fraiche
- 1 onion (Chopped)
- ½ cup Parmesan (Grated)
- 1 cup risotto rice
- 1 cup zucchini (Diced)
- 1 vegetable stock cube
- 2 sprigs lemon thyme
- juice and zest of 1 lemon

Directions:

1. Add the butter to a skillet, and melt it, then add the onion and fry on a low heat for 5-8 minutes, or until it's soft.
2. Now add the garlic and cook for 1 minute.

3. Add the rice, and stir it well so the butter and onions coat it. Cook for another 2 minutes.
4. Now take the stock cube, and dissolve in in 1 liter of boiling water.
5. Add 1 ladle of the stock to the rice, and then add the thyme and lemon juice, and stir.
6. Cook on a medium heat stirring all the time. Do this until all the liquid is absorbed, Now add the zucchini, and stir well, then repeat with another ladle of stock, an continue until you've used all the stock up, and it's all been absorbed, and the rice is creamy.
7. Add the lemon zest crème fraiche and Parmesan.

Chinese-Style Pork
Makes: 4 servings

Ingredients
- 1 lbs. Pork fillet
- ¾ cup scallions (Sliced)
- 2 ½ cups chicken stock
- 1 tsp chili flakes
- 1 tbsp. soy sauce
- 2 cups baby leaf greens
- 2 tsp Chinese spice mix
- 2 tbsp. ginger (Peeled, finely chopped)

Directions:
1. Add all of the ingredients apart from the green and scallions into a sauce pot, and the lid, and allow to simmer on a medium-high heat.

2. Cook for 8-10 minutes, or until the pork is slightly cooked, and the greens are completely done.
3. Sprinkle the scallions on top.

Coconut Rice & Salmon

Makes: 6 servings

Ingredients

- ½ cup cilantro
- 1 red chili (Seeded, chopped)
- 3 limes
- 4 scallions (Thinly sliced)
- 2 cans coconut milk
- 2 tsp golden sugar
- 2 tbsp. olive oil
- 3 tbsp. soy sauce
- small scoop butter
- 6 salmon fillets (Skinless)
- 2 shallots (Chopped)
- 4 lime leaves
- 1 cup Thai red curry paste
- 2 ½ cups basmati rice

Directions:

1. Grate the zest of 1 lime, and set to one side. Now add the coconut milk to a bowl, and fill one of the cans with water, and pour this into the bowl.
2. Set to one side. Heat the butter and oil in a skillet on a low heat, and add the shallots. Cook for about 5 minutes, or until the shallots are slightly golden.
3. Add the curry paste, and cook for 1 more minutes.
4. Remove the skillet from the heat, and then add the cilantro, rice, tsp salt, and lime zest.
5. Mix well, and then pour the coconut milk on top. Stir well, and then add back to the heat, and simmer on a medium heat for a few minutes.
6. Add the lime leaves, stir, and simmer for 5 more minutes.
7. Stir the rice, then place the salmon on top of the rice. Cover, and simmer on a low heat for up to 20 minutes, or until the salmon is cooked.
8. Now squeeze the juice out of 2 of the limes, and add the sugar and soy sauce to it, and mix well.
9. Add the scallions, cilantro and chili, and chop the remaining lime into wedges.

10. Take the rice and fish off the heat, and set to one side for 5 minutes. After 5 minutes, make your servings.

11. Add 1/3 of the salad to each portion/pot add the coconut rice, place a salmon fillet on top, and sprinkle the dressing on.

12. Add a lime wedge on top of that.

Quinoa and Kale Salad with Almonds and Orange Dressing

Makes: 3 servings

Ingredients

- ½ tbsp. olive oil
- ¼ cup whole almonds (Roasted, salted, chopped)
- ½ onion (Diced)
- ¼ cup dates (Pitted)
- Salt
- ½ bunch kale (Sliced)
- ¼ cup red quinoa
- ½ garlic clove (Crushed)
- Juice of ½ Mandarin orange
- Salt & pepper
- Juice of ¼ lime
- 1 tsp maple syrup

Directions:

1. Heat the oil in a skillet, and add the onion, and a bit of salt. Cook on a medium heat for 20 minutes, or until the onion is caramelized.

2. Set to one side. Add the garlic and quinoa to a sauce pot, and cook on a medium heat for 1 minute to toast to quinoa.

3. Add ½ tsp salt and 1 cup water, and allow to boil. Now place the lid on the pot.

4. And cook for 12-15 minutes, then turn the heat off, but leave the lid on for 5 more minutes, then fluff the quinoa with a fork.

5. Add the lime and orange juice to a bowl, and mix them together well. Now add the oil and syrup, and mix again.

6. Add 2 tbsp. of this dressing to the quinoa, and mix well. Now add the kale to the quinoa, along with the onions, and mix well.

7. Add half of the remaining dressing and mix well again. Add the almonds and dates, season, and add the rest of the dressing if you wish.

Sweet Potato Wraps with Onions & Pesto

Makes: 4-5 servings

Ingredients

- 1 ½ sweet potatoes (Cubed)
- Olive oil
- ¼ cup pesto
- 1/3 cup Parmesan (Grated)
- 1 ½ Portobello mushrooms (Sliced)
- 1 pint small tomatoes (Halved)
- 4-5 wraps
- 1 yellow onion (Peeled, sliced)

Directions:

1. Preheat your oven to 400 Fahrenheit, and line 2 baking sheets.
2. Add the tomatoes, mushrooms and sweet potatoes to the sheet, and drizzle the olive oil over them, and season.
3. Toss well, and then spread them out. Add to the oven and cook for 35-45 minutes, or until the mushrooms and tomatoes are soft, and the potatoes are a little brown.
4. Heat a skillet, and add the onions and 1 tbsp. olive oil. Cook on a medium heat for until the onions are soft.
5. Add some water to deglaze the plan, if the skillet is getting dry. Set to one side.
6. Now place the wraps in a skillet, and warm them for about 10 seconds.
7. Spread 2 tsp pesto on each wrap, and add some mushrooms, potatoes, tomatoes and onions, along with some Parmesan to each wrap.
8. Close the wrap.

Parmesan Chicken with Roasted Romaine Lettuce
Makes: 4 servings

Ingredients

- 4 chicken breasts (Boneless, skinless)
- 1 lemon (Chopped into wedges)
- Salt & pepper

- 4 anchovy fillets (Chopped)
- ½ cup Parmesan (Grated)
- 2 hearts romaine lettuce (Chopped lengthwise)
- ½ cup breadcrumbs
- 2 cloves garlic (Chopped)
- 3 tbsp. extra virgin olive oil
- 2 tbsp. parsley

Directions:

1. Preheat your oven to 450 Fahrenheit, and then line a baking sheet with foil. Season the chicken, and add it to the sheet.
2. Now add the rest of the ingredients apart from the anchovies, and lemon wedges 1 tbsp. oil, and 1 garlic clove to a bowl, and mix well.
3. Take the mixture in your hands, and pat it gently onto the chicken. Add to the oven and cook for 10 minutes, or until the crumbs are golden brown.
4. Now drizzle the remaining oil over the lettuce, and sprinkle the rest of the garlic on top.
5. Season, and then add the chicken to the baking sheet, Cook for about 10 minutes, or until the chicken is thoroughly cooked, and the lettuce has started to go a little brown at the edges.
6. Top with the anchovies, and place the lemon wedges around the edges.

Middle-Eastern Wrap
Makes: 1 serving

Ingredients

- ½ cup romaine lettuce (Shredded)
- 3 dolmas
- ¼ cup cucumber (Chopped)
- 1 wrap
- ¼ cup tomato (Chopped)
- 1/8 tsp garlic powder
- ¼ cup plain yogurt
- 1 tbsp. feta cheese

Directions:

1. Add the garlic, feta, cucumber, yogurt, lettuce and tomato to a bowl, and mix well.
2. Spread this mixture onto the wrap, and add the dolmas on top.
3. Roll up the wrap.

Spicy Chicken & Sweet Potato
Makes: 6 serving

Ingredients

- 2 lbs. boneless skinless chicken breasts cut into small pieces
- Seasoning mix: more or less to taste and preference

- 1 tsp garlic
- ½ tsp paprika
- ½ tsp cayenne
- ½ tsp red pepper flakes
- Salt and pepper
- 2 tbsp. olive oil
- 3 sweet potatoes peeled and diced
- 5-6 cups broccoli cut up
- Salt and pepper
- Avocado/hummus/lemon juice/chives/olive oil for serving.

Directions:

1. Preheat oven to 425 degrees. Toss chicken with bit of olive oil and the seasoning mix.
2. Let marinate in fridge for 30 minutes while you prepare the rest of ingredients.
3. Arrange sweet potatoes and broccoli on their own sheet pans and drizzle with olive oil and salt.
4. Place chicken on separate sheet pan. Bake all for 12-15 minutes and then remove broccoli and chicken.
5. Stir sweet potatoes and continue roasting for another 15 minutes. Divide into containers and enjoy!

Curried Chicken Pita Pockets

Makes: 4 servings

Ingredients

- 6 tbsp. plain yogurt
- 2 cups sprouts
- ¼ cup mayonnaise
- 4 pita breads
- 1 tbsp. curry powder
- ¼ cup almonds (Sliced, toasted)
- 2 cups chicken breast (Cubed)
- ½ cup dried cranberries
- 1 pear (Diced)
- 1 celery stalk (Diced)

Directions:

1. Add the mayonnaise, curry powder and yogurt to a bowl, and mix well.
2. Now add the rest of the ingredients apart from the sprouts.
3. Mix well, and then fill the pita pockets with the chicken mix.
4. Add the sprouts on top, and close the pockets as much as you can.

Chicken, Cilantro Cheese, Pepper Taquitos

Ingredients:

- 8 ounces cream cheese
- 3 cups roasted chicken breast, shredded (or roast beef)

- 1 can (6 ounces) green chilies
- 1 teaspoon onion powder
- 1/4 teaspoon garlic powder
- 2 tablespoons lime juice
- 3/4 teaspoon cumin
- 4 tablespoons cilantro, chopped
- 1 1/2 teaspoon chili powder
- 1 1/2 cups pepper jack cheese, shredded
- Cooking spray
- Fine sea salt
- Small-sized corn or flour tortillas

Directions:

1. Melt the cream cheese until melty and soft.
2. Put all the spices, lime juice, cilantro, chicken, green chilies, and cheese inside a large-sized bowl; mix well until blended well.
3. Heat the tortillas until pliable and soft.
4. Add about 2 tablespoons of the chicken mix into each tortilla; roll the tortillas, and, with the seam side down, put them on a cookie sheet lined with parchment paper or foil. Spray with a bit of olive oil spray and then sprinkle with a bit of salt; bake in a 425F oven for 15 minutes.
5. Freezing: If making ahead of time, arrange the rolls on the cookie sheet without touching each other. Flash freeze in the freezer until frozen. Transfer into a gallon-sized freezer bag, label, and keep in the freezer.

6. When ready to eat, take out needed serving and put in a cookie sheet lined with foil or parchment paper. Spray lightly with olive oil and then sprinkle with a bit of salt; bake at 425F for about 15 to 20 minutes or till crispy.

Cheesy Ham Sliders

Ingredients:

- 1 pound deli ham, more or less
- 7 ounces Swiss cheese slices
- 15-20 mini wheat rolls
- 1/3 cup brown sugar
- 1/2 cup butter
- 1 tablespoon Worcestershire
- 1 tablespoon poppy seeds
- 1 tablespoon mustard

Directions:

1. Preheat the oven to 350F.
2. Sandwich folded 1-2 slices ham and 1/2 slice cheese between each roll. Put the sandwiches side by side into a 9x13-inch baking dish or whatever size you have.
3. In a medium-sized saucepan, mix the butter with the Worcestershire sauce, mustard, brown sugar substitute, and poppy seeds; bring the mix to a boil over medium-high heat; when boiling reduce the heat. Lightly drizzle each sandwich with the sauce.
4. Cover the baking dish with foil and then bake for about 20 minutes.

Cheesy Bean Burritos

Ingredients:

- 8 tortillas, burrito size, about 8 1/2-inch across
- 4 ounces mild cheddar cheese, freshly grated (about 1 cup)
- 2 cans (16 ounces) refried beans
- 1 medium sweet yellow onion, diced

Directions:

1. Cut 8 pieces 12x12-inch pieces of foil and wax paper.
2. Top each tortilla with 1/3 cup of refried beans, 2 tablespoons of cheddar cheese, and 2 tablespoons of onions.
3. Wrap each burrito tortilla around each filling. Wrap each burrito with a wax paper and then with a foil.

Chicken Poblano Soup

Ingredients:

- 4 cups chicken broth or stock
- 3/4 cups onion, diced
- 2 1/2 cups boneless chicken breasts, diced
- 1/4 cups lime juice
- 1/4 cups fresh cilantro, chopped
- 1/2 tablespoons chili powder
- 1/2 cups poblano pepper, seeded and diced
- 1 tablespoon cumin

Directions:

1. Inside a large-sized stockpot, combine the chicken broth with the onion, poblano peppers, chili powder, and cumin; bring to a boil.
2. Add the chicken, lime juice, and cilantro; reduce the heat to a simmer. Cover and cook for 30 minutes.

Homemade Hot Pockets

Ingredients:

- 4 cups flour
- 1 1/2 cups cheddar cheese
- 1 1/2 cups mozzarella cheese
- 1 1/2 cups warm water
- 1 1/2 tablespoon yeast
- 1 1/2 teaspoon salt
- 2 1/2 cups ham or pepperoni, chopped
- 3 tablespoons olive oil
- Pizza sauce (for the pizza hot pockets)

Directions:

1. Put the flour, yeast, and salt into a food processor with the blade attachment; pulse until well mixed. Add the olive oil, pulsing in.
2. Turn the motor of the food processor on. With the motor running, pour in the warm water; let the machine run until the dough pulls away from the edges and forms a ball.
3. Put the dough into a greased bowl and then cover; let rise until the size is doubled.
4. Take out a handful of dough; roll into a small circle, about the size of your hand.
5. Add some meat and cheese into the dough circle; fold to make a half circle. Seal the edges and put on an ungreased cookie sheet. Repeat
6. The process with the remaining dough, meat, and cheese.
7. Preheat the oven to 450F. Bake the pockets for about 12 to 15 minutes.

Chicken Salsa Pockets

Ingredients:

For the dough:

- 1 1/4 cup unbleached flour
- 1 1/4 cup whole-wheat flour
- 1 cup warm water (105-115F)
- 1 tablespoon active dry yeast
- 1 teaspoon salt
- 1 teaspoon sugar
- 2 tablespoons olive oil

For the filling:

- 1-2 cups chicken, baked and then chopped
- 1 1/2 cups cheese, shredded
- 1/2 cup salsa

Directions:

1. Mix the yeast with the warm water until dissolved. Add the sugar, oil, salt, and the flour; mix well and then put the dough on a floured working surface. Knead for about 3 to 5 minutes or till the dough is soft.

2. Divide the dough into 10 portions. Roll each portion into balls and then with a rolling pin, flatten the balls into circles. Put a spoonful

salsa into each dough circle and sprinkle with chicken and cheese; fold over and then tightly seal.

3. Put on a greased cookie sheet and bake at 500F for about 10-15 minutes or till browned.

Shrimp and Cheese Tortillas

Ingredients:

- 2 bags (2 pounds each) frozen raw shrimp
- 12 pieces (10-inch) flour tortillas
- 1 pound Gouda cheese, shredded
- 1 tablespoon garlic, finely chopped
- 1 lemon, halved
- 2 tablespoons butter
- 3 chipotle chilies in adobo sauce, plus 1 tsp adobo sauce
- Salt and pepper, to taste

Directions:

1. Inside a large-sized, deep skillet, melt the butter over medium-high heat.
2. Add the shrimp, garlic, 1/2 teaspoon of pepper, and 1/2 teaspoon of salt. Increase the heat to thigh; cook, stirring frequently, for about 4 minutes or till the shrimps are just opaque. Squeeze the lemon halves over the shrimps; remove from heat and set aside.
3. In a small-sized bowl, mash the chipotles with the adobo sauce until a paste. Spread a thin layer of the paste on each tortilla. Cover 1/2 of

each tortilla with a single layer shrimp; sprinkle with the cheese and then fold the other half over the filling.

4. Working in batches, cook 2 quesadillas; place them on the skillet with the cheese side down Inside a large-sized nonstick skillet and cook on medium-high heat for about 2 minutes per side, or until golden. Cut the quesadillas into wedges.

Mini Italian Burgers

Ingredients:

- 1 1/2-1 3/4 pounds ground beef
- 1 clove garlic, peeled and then minced
- 1 teaspoon salt
- 1/2 cup Parmesan, freshly grated
- 1/3 cup fresh flat-leaf parsley, finely chopped
- 1/4 teaspoon black pepper, freshly ground
- 2 tablespoons tomato paste
- 4 slices Provolone or mozzarella cheese
- 8 mini buns, sliced into halves

Optional toppings:

- Ketchup
- Lettuce
- Mayonnaise
- Tomato slices

Directions:

1. Grease a pan and preheat on medium heat. Alternatively, you can preheat a charcoal or a gas grill.

2. Put the ground beef, parsley, garlic, tomato paste, parmesan cheese, salt, and pepper into a mixing bowl. With clean hands, combine the ingredients until well mixed, making sure not to compress the ingredients.

3. Divide the mix into 8 portions and shape into equal thickness and size patties.

4. Put the burgers on the pan or on the grill; cook for about 3 to 4 minutes per side or until cooked through.

5. Top each warm burger with 1/2 slice of cheese; serve on buns with your toppings of choice.

Slow Cooked Balsamic Beef

Ingredients:

- 1 tablespoon soy sauce
- 3-4 pound roast beef, boneless
- 1/4 cup balsamic vinegar
- 2 teaspoons steak seasoning, all natural
- 1/2 teaspoon red pepper flakes
- 4 cloves garlic, minced
- 1 tablespoon Worcestershire sauce
- 1 cup beef broth
- 1 tablespoon honey

Directions:

1. Put the roast beef in a slow cooker.
2. In a small-sized bowl, mix the remaining ingredients together until combined; pour over the roast beef.
3. Cook on LOW for about 8 hours or until the meat shreds easily apart.
4. With 2 forks, shred the beef meat apart in the slow cooker.
5. Serve warm on top of mashed potatoes or in buns with a little sauce over the top.

Chicken, Black Bean Enchiladas

Ingredients:

- 1 1/3 cups Monterey Jack and or Cheddar cheese
- 1 can black beans, rinsed and then drained
- 1 can (4-ounce) diced green chilies
- 1 pound boneless, skinless chicken breasts, cut
- 1/2-1 cup red enchilada sauce
- 1/3 cup salsa, prepared mild, medium, or hot
- 1/4 cup onion, chopped
- 2 cloves garlic, minced
- 2 teaspoons olive oil
- 4-6 pieces (8-inch) whole-wheat tortillas
- Homemade taco seasoning

Directions:

1. Preheat the oven to 400F. Grease a 9x9-inch casserole dish with cooking spray.
2. Inside a large-sized skillet, heat the oil over medium heat.
3. Add the garlic and the onion, sauté for 2 minutes.

4. Add the chicken; sauté for about 5 minutes or till cooked through and golden brown. Add the taco seasoning.

5. Stir in the black beans, salsa, and green chilies; simmer for about 5 minutes or till the sauce is reduced and thick.

6. Put 1/2 of the enchilada sauce into the bottom of the prepared dish.

7. Arrange 6 tortillas on a clean, flat surface. Divide the chicken-bean mix between each tortilla and top each with about 1 to 2 tablespoons of cheese. Roll each tortilla, and with the seam side down, put side by side in the baking dish. Drizzle the remaining enchilada sauce over the rolled tortillas. Sprinkle with the remaining cheese.

8. Bake in the oven for about 15 minutes or till the cheese topping is golden.

Asian Lettuce Wraps

Ingredients:

- 16 Boston Bibb, butter leaf, or lettuce leaves
- 1 pound ground chicken, lean (or turkey or beef)
- 1 can (8 ounces) water chestnuts, drained
- 1 cup cabbage, shredded
- 1 cup carrots, shredded
- 1 large yellow onion, finely chopped
- 1 tablespoon cooking oil

- 1/2 bunch green onions, chopped
- 1/2 cup hoisin sauce
- 2 cloves fresh garlic, minced
- 2 tablespoons rice wine vinegar
- 2 tablespoons soy sauce, or to taste
- 2 teaspoons freshly grated ginger
- Asian Chile pepper sauce
- 4 teaspoons Asian (dark) sesame oil
- 2 cups brown rice, cooked, optional

Directions:

1. Rinse the whole lettuce leaves clean and then pat dry carefully so you don't tear them; set aside.
2. Inside a large skillet or in a pot, brown the chicken with 1 tablespoon of oil, frequently stirring. When browned, drain excess grease and set aside to cool.
3. In the same pan, sauté the yellow onion over medium heat, stirring frequently, until tender. Add the garlic, hoisin sauce, soy sauce, rice wine, ginger, and the chili pepper; stir to combine and simmer for 1 to 2 minutes.
4. Stir in the green onions, water chestnuts, cabbage, carrots, browned chicken, and sesame oil; continue cooking for about 3 to 4 minutes or till carrots, cabbage, and onion just start to soften. If the mix seems to

4. Dry, just add more hoisin and/or soy sauce to taste; add carefully or it can become too salty.

5. To serve, spoon the chicken mix into a lettuce leaf, wrap it like a burrito, and enjoy.

Chicken, Mozzarella Cheese Fajitas

Ingredients:

- 1 1/2 cups mozzarella cheese, shredded
- 1 can corn (or 5-6 ears of roasted corn)
- 2-3 chicken breasts (4 ounces each), cooked and diced
- 2 tablespoons olive oil
- 2 garlic cloves, minced
- 1/2 onion, chopped
- 1/2 cup salsa
- 1 tablespoon taco seasoning
- 1 red bell pepper, small-medium, diced
- 1 green bell pepper, small-medium, diced
- 8 tortillas, medium-sized

Directions:

1. Preheat the oven to 400F.
2. Grease a 9x9-inch casserole dish and a 9x12-inch dish with cooking spray.
3. Inside a large-sized skillet, heat the oil over medium heat. Add the garlic and the onion; sauté for about 1 to 2 minutes. Add the bell peppers; continue cooking for about 5 to 7 minutes or till starting to soften.

4. Add the chicken, corn, and the salsa. Sprinkle taco seasoning all over; toss until well combined. Remove from the heat.

5. Lay a tortilla out on a clean surface; sprinkle with some shredded cheese. Add a generous 1/2 cup of chicken filling; roll the tortilla and with the same side down, put into the prepared dishes. Repeat the process with the remaining tortilla, cheese, and filling.

6. Sprinkle the top with a generous amount of shredded cheese; bake at 400F for about 15 minutes or till the cheese is melted.

Chicken Burritos

Ingredients:

- 3/4 cup frozen corn
- 3/4 cup cooked black beans
- 3/4 cup brown rice, cooked
- 2/3 cups water
- 2 pieces chicken breasts, diced
- 1-2 tablespoons olive oil
- 1/2-1 cup mild salsa (adjust to taste)
- 1 packet store-bought mild taco seasoning
- 1 1/2 cups shredded cheddar cheese
- 8 pieces (8-inch) whole wheat tortillas

Optional toppings:

- Guacamole or creamy avocado dip
- Sour cream or plain Greek yogurt

- Pico de Gallo

Directions:

1. Inside a large-sized skillet, heat 1-2 tablespoons of olive oil on medium to medium-high heat. Add the chicken, sauté for about 3 to 4 minutes or till cooked through.

2. Add the water, salsa, brown rice, corn, black beans, and taco seasoning; reduce the heat to low and simmer for 5 minutes, occasionally stirring.

3. To assemble the burritos, put a generous 1/3 cup of meat mix and 3 tablespoons of shredded cheese on each tortilla. Pull in each end and then roll up tightly.

4. If serving immediately, wrap each tortilla with foil, heat in a 350F oven for about 15-20 minutes. Alternatively, you can wrap each tortilla with

4. Moist paper towel; warm in 30-second increments in the microwave until heated through. Serve with the optional toppings, if desired.

Chicken and Bacon Sandwiches

Ingredients:

- 3 large boneless, skinless chicken breasts
- 3 tablespoons cider vinegar
- 6 slices bacon, cooked and then broken in halves
- 6 slices cheddar cheese
- 6 tablespoons olive oil
- 1 tablespoon salt
- 1 tablespoon garlic powder
- 1 1/2 teaspoon powdered ginger
- 1 1/2 teaspoon paprika
- 1 1/2 teaspoon ground black pepper
- 6 hamburger whole-wheat buns

Optional toppings:

- Lettuce
- Tomato slices
- Onion slices
- Mayonnaise

- Dijon mustard

Directions:

1. Into a gallon-sized freezer bag, combine the oil with the vinegar, salt, pepper, garlic powder, paprika, and ginger. Gently shake the bag to mix and set aside.
2. Carefully cut the chicken breast lengthwise, cutting through the center to make 2 thin chicken breast halves.
3. Put the chicken breast halves into the freezer with marinade, seal, and shake to coat the meat.
4. Put the bag in the fridge and let marinate for at least 15 minutes or up to several hours.
5. Preheat a grill or a grill pan to medium-high heat.

6. Lightly grease the grill or grill pan with cooking spray. Put the chicken on the pan or grill; discard the marinade.

7. Grill for about 3-4 minutes or till there are prominent grill marks on the bottom.

8. Carefully flip the chicken. Reduce the heat to medium, cover the pan/grill; grill for another 3-4 minutes or till cooked through.

9. The chicken is done when the internal temperature is 165F and the meat juices run clear.

10. Sandwich 1 chicken, 1 cheese, 1 bacon cut into 3 pieces, and your choice of optional toppings in the buns.

Dinner

Skillet Sausage and Shrimp
Ingredients:

2 bags (2 pounds) shrimp, raw, frozen (31-40 per pound)

1 can (14 1/2 ounces) diced tomatoes

4 links chicken apple sausage, precooked, cut into 1-inch pieces

4 cups long-grain white rice

2 teaspoons garlic, finely chopped

2 tablespoons butter

1/4 cup extra-virgin olive oil

1 large onion, chopped

1 large green bell pepper, chopped

6 cups chicken broth

Salt and pepper

Directions:

- Inside a large-sized, deep skillet, heat the butter and the olive oil on medium-high heat.
- Add the rice and the onion; cook, occasionally stirring, for about 5 minutes or till the onion is soft.
- Add the garlic, bell pepper, and the sausage; cook, stirring, for about 3 minutes or till the veggies are soft.
- Remove from the heat, stir in the tomatoes along with their juices; season with salt and pepper to taste. Let completely.
- Divide the rice mix into3 portions, put into 3 re-sealable 1 gallon-sized freezer bags, and pour 2 cups chicken broth into each freezer bag, label, and freeze.
- Divide the shrimp into 3 portions, put into 3 resalable, 1 gallon-sized freezer bags, label, and freeze.
- When ready to serve, take out a portion of the rice mix and the shrimp from the freezer. Put the shrimp in a large bowl of cold water and let thaw.
- Put the frozen rice mix into a skillet; heat the skillet, thawing the mix and then bring to a boil. When boiling, lower the heat, cover the skillet, and simmer for about 17 minutes or till the rice is tender.

- Drain the thawed shrimp. Add to the rice mix; cook on medium heat, frequently stirring, for about 5 minutes or till the shrimp is opaque. Serve.

Cheddar Cheesy Beef Potpie

Ingredients:

1 1/2 pounds ground beef

1 1/2 cups flour

1 can (28 ounces) diced tomatoes, drained

1 cup beef broth

1 small onion, chopped

1/2 cup milk

2 cups sharp cheddar cheese, shredded (8 ounces)

2 teaspoons baking powder

6 tablespoons butter, chilled

Salt and pepper

Directions:

- Preheat the oven to 375F. Grease an 8x12-inch baking dish; set aside.
- Heat 2 tablespoons of butter inside a large-sized skillet over medium high heat. Add onion; cook for about 3-5 minutes, stirring, until soft.
- Add the beef; cook, crumbling with the back of a spoon, for about 5 minutes or till no longer pink.

- Stir in the beef broth and the tomatoes; season with salt and pepper to taste.
- Lower the heat; cook, occasionally stirring, for about 20 minutes or till most of the liquid has evaporated. Pour the mix into the greased baking dish, spreading evenly.
- Inside a large-sized bowl, combine the flour with the baking powder and 1/2 teaspoon salt.
- With a pastry blender or your fingertips, blend the remaining 4 tablespoons of butter and cheese into the flour mix until the mix resembles coarse crumbs.
- Pour the milk in; quickly stir using a fork to from a dry, shaggy dough.
- Gather the dough together and knead lightly inside the bowl.
- Transfer to a floured surface; pat or roll the dough into a large 1/2-inch thick round.
- With a 3-inch cookie cutter, cut out 8 biscuits from the dough. Gather the leftover dough and again shape into 1/2-inch thick round; cut out more biscuits.
- Repeat the process until all the dough is used.

- ■

- Put the biscuits on top of the beef mixture, placing them as close together as possible; bake for about 35 minutes or till the biscuits are lightly browned.

Cheeseburger Meatloaf with Mashed Potatoes

Ingredients:

1 1/2 pounds ground beef

1/2 cup bread-and-butter pickle chips, chopped

2 large eggs

2 pounds new red potatoes

8 ounces cheddar cheese, cut into 1/3-inch cubes

3/4 cup heavy cream

2/3 cup ketchup

2/3 cup breadcrumbs

1 red onion, finely chopped

2 tablespoons extra-virgin olive oil, plus more for greasing

Directions:

- Preheat the oven to 400F. Lightly grease a rimmed baking sheet; set aside.
- Heat 2 tablespoons of olive oil in a medium-sized skillet over medium heat. Add the onion, cook, stirring for about 3 minutes or till soft.
- Inside a large-sized bowl, combine the ketchup with the eggs, breadcrumbs, and pickles. Mix the onion into the ketchup mix.
- Crumble the beef and the cheese; mix together with the ketchup mix. Transfer the beef mix into the greased baking sheet.

- Shape into a 4x12inch loaf; bake for about 35 minutes or till reach 160F when inserted into the center of the loaf.
- While the meatloaf is cooking, cut the potatoes into halves. Put them inside a large-sized pot.
- Pour water to cover the potatoes by 1 inch. Salt the water and bring to a boil. When boiling, reduce the heat to a simmer; cook for about 10 to 15 minutes or until tender.
- Drain and then return the potatoes to the pot. Mash with the cream.
- When the meatloaf is cooked, let rest for 5 minutes, slice, and serve with the mashed potatoes.

Beef Lasagna Ravioli Bake
Ingredients:

1 can (15 ounces) crushed Italian tomatoes

1 pounds ground beef (preferably grass-fed, organic)

1/2 medium-sized onion, diced

1/2 pounds pork sausage (preferably local, organic)

2 cups Italian mix cheese, shredded (Romano, Parmesan, Asiago, etc.)

2 cups mozzarella cheese, shredded

2 jars (28 ounces each) spaghetti sauce

2 packages (10 ounces each) fresh cheese ravioli, cooked al dente

2-3 garlic cloves, minced

Grated Parmesan cheese, for serving, optional

Directions:

- Preheat the oven to 375F. Grease a 9x13-inch baking pan with cooking spray.
- Inside a large-sized skillet, sauté the onions over medium heat until soft. Add the garlic; sauté for 1 minute, making sure it does not burn.
- Add the beef and the sausage; increase the heat to medium-high. Cook until the beef is no longer pink and the sausage is browned.
- Drain the grease. Stir in the sauce and the crushed tomatoes; remove the skillet from the heat.
- Spread a thin layer of the meat sauce onto the bottom of the baking dish.
- Arrange a layer of cooked ravioli over the sauce, sprinkle with the mozzarella cheese and the Italian cheese.
- Repeat the layers with the sauce as the final top layer. Cover the baking dish with the foil; bake for 45 minutes or till heated through.
- Remove the foil and bake for another 15 minutes or till the edges are bubbly. Let rest for 10 minutes, slice, sprinkle with parmesan cheese and serve.

Baked Italian Meatballs
Ingredients:

      1 1/2 pounds ground beef (or ground turkey)

      1 cup whole-wheat breadcrumbs (or panko)

      1 large egg, beaten

      1 teaspoon salt

      1/2 teaspoon garlic powder

      1/2 teaspoon ground pepper

      1/2 teaspoon Italian seasoning

      1/4 cup fresh parsley, finely chopped, loosely packed

      2 tablespoons milk

      2 tablespoons tomato paste

Directions:

- Preheat the oven to 350F. Line a sheet pan with foil or with parchment paper.
- With clean hands, gently combine all the ingredients in a medium sized bowl.
- With a spoon or a medium-sized dough scooper, scoop and roll the mix into 1 1/2-inch meatballs.
- Line the meatballs on the prepared sheet pan, leaving a space between each; bake for about 20 minutes or till the inside is no longer pink or the internal temperature is 160F.

Slow Cooked Pot Roast

Ingredients:

4-6 medium russet potatoes, chopped into 1-inch pieces (or about 5-7 cups)

4 celery stalks, chopped

3-5 large carrots, chopped into 1-inch pieces (or about 2 cups)

3 garlic cloves, minced

2-3 pounds rump roast (trim off visible fat)

2 tablespoons whole-wheat flour

2 onions, diced

1/4 teaspoon garlic powder

1/4 teaspoon black pepper

1/4 cup red wine

1/2 teaspoon salt

1 tablespoon Italian seasoning

1 cup low sodium chicken stock

1 can (8 ounces) no-salt tomato sauce

1 bay leaf

All-natural steak seasoning

Olive oil

Salt and pepper

Directions:

- In a skillet, heat a couple tablespoons of olive oil on medium-high heat.
- Season all the sides of the roast with the seasoning steaks. Put in the skillet and brown all sides, about 2 minutes each side.
- Put the browned roast into the slow cooker.
- Add a bit more oil to the skillet, if necessary. Add the celery, onion, and garlic; sauté for about 3 to 5 minutes or until tender.
- Season with salt and pepper while sautéing and with a wooden spoon, scrape the browned bits from the bottom of the pan.
- Meanwhile, in a medium-mixing bowl, whisk the tomato sauce with the chicken stock, red wine, Italian seasoning, bay leaf, black pepper,

- Garlic powder, salt, and whole-wheat flour; pour the mix into the slow cooker.
- Add the celery mix into the slow cooker; stir to mix and coat the meat and the veggies with the sauce.
- Slow cook for about 4 to 5 hours on LOW, or, if desired, longer.
- Add the potatoes and the carrots into the sauce; cook for 2 hours more or until the veggies are tender.
- Remove the roast, let rest for about 10 minutes on a wooden cutting board.
- Turn off the slow cooker, remove the lid, and allow to rest. With 2 forks, shred the roast and then gently stir in the veggie and the sauce in the cooker.
- Adjust the seasoning, if desired.

Casserole Chicken Parmesan

Ingredients:

4 cups chicken, fully cooked, shredded or cubed

1-2 tablespoons olive oil

1/2 cup Parmesan cheese, shredded or grated

1 jar (28 ounces) marinara sauce

1 cup whole-wheat breadcrumbs (or panko)

1 1/2 cups mozzarella cheese, shredded

Fresh herbs, chopped (oregano, basil, parsley, etc.), to taste

Salt and pepper, to taste

Directions:

- Preheat the oven to 350F. Grease an 8x8-inch dish with cooking spray.
- Layer the chicken onto the bottom of the dish. Pour the marinara sauce over; mix until the chicken is coated.
- Top with the cheeses until the chicken is covered.
- In a small-sized bowl, mix the breadcrumbs with the fresh herbs olive oil, dash salt, and dash pepper; sprinkle the seasoned crumbs over the top.
- Bake for about 20 to 25 minutes or till the top is golden and the sides are bubbling.

Lemon Chicken Picasa

Ingredients:

4 pieces (4 ounces each) boneless, skinless chicken breasts

2/3 cup lemon juice, freshly squeezed (2 lemons), lemon halves reserved

2 extra-large eggs

1/2 cup whole-wheat flour

1 tablespoon water

1 cup dry white wine (choose one that you'd drink)

1 1/2 cups whole-wheat breadcrumbs (or panko)

6 tablespoons unsalted butter, room temperature, divided

Fresh parsley, chopped, for serving

Olive oil

Kosher salt and freshly ground black pepper

Sliced lemon, for serving

Directions:

- Preheat the oven to 400F. Line a sheet pan with parchment paper.
- Put each chicken breast between 2 sheets of plastic wrap or parchment paper; pound to ¼-inch thickness and then season both sides with salt and pepper.

- In a shallow plate; mix the flour with ½ teaspoon of pepper and 1 teaspoon of salt.
- In another plate, beat the eggs with 1 tablespoon of water.
- Pour the breadcrumbs into a third plate.
- Dip each chicken breast into the flour; shake off excess. Dip in the egg and then in the breadcrumb mix.
- Heat 2 tablespoons of olive oil inside a large-sized sauté pan over medium to medium-low heat.
- Working 2 breasts at a time, put chicken into the pan; cook for 2 minutes per side or until browned. Put the browned chickens on the sheet pan.
- Wipe the pan clean. Put 2 tablespoons olive oil, heat, and then cook the remaining chicken breasts as directed above; put on the sheet pan.
- Bake for about 5-10 minutes or till the insides of the chickens is no longer pink.

- Meanwhile, wipe the sauté pan clean using dry paper towel. Melt the butter in a pan over medium heat. Add the lime juice, the wine, reserved lemon halves, 1/2 teaspoon of pepper, and 1 teaspoon of salt; bring to boil over high heat for about 2 to 3 minutes or till reduced by half. Turn the heat off, add the remaining 4 tablespoons of butter; swirl to combine. Discard the lemon halves.
- Serve 1 chicken breast on each plate; spoon the sauce over the chickens. Serve with a lemon slice and a sprinkle of fresh parsley.

Parmesan Chicken Tenders

Ingredients:

1 1/3 pounds chicken tenders

1 1/2 teaspoons Old Bay seasoning

1/2 teaspoon garlic powder

1/4 cup Parmesan cheese, finely grated

1/4 cup whole-wheat flour

2 tablespoons olive oil

Salt and pepper

Directions:

- Preheat the oven to 425F.

- Cover a metal sheet pan with foil. Put the pan into the preheated oven to heat.
- Put the flour, Old Bay seasoning, parmesan, and garlic powder inside a large-sized Ziploc plastic bag; shake until well combined and set aside.
- In a small-sized bowl, lightly season the chicken tenders with the salt and the pepper and then toss with the olive oil coated.
- Several chicken tenders at a time, add into the bag with the flour mix; seal and shake until each piece are coated.
- Carefully remove the hot sheet pan from the oven; generously grease with the cooking spray.
- Arrange the seasoned chicken tenders in the pan, arranging with a space between each piece; bake at 425F for about 15 minutes or till the chicken tenders are done, turning once halfway baking.
- The chicken is done when the insides are no longer pink or the internal temperature 165F.
- Serve immediately.

Chicken Parmesan

Ingredients:

4 chicken breasts, pounded out to about ½ inch thickness

2/3 cup Italian seasoned breadcrumbs

1/3 cup Parmesan cheese

1 egg, lightly beaten

1 cup mozzarella cheese

1 cup marinara sauce

Salt and pepper

Splash milk

Directions:

- Preheat oven to 350F.
- Grease a 9x13 baking pan or dish with cooking spray or rub with a vegetable; set aside.
- Put the chicken breasts between sheets of plastic wrap. With the flat side of the meat mallet or with the bottom of a glass or heavy pan, pound into 1/2-inch thick
- Sprinkle both sides of the chicken breasts with a pinch of salt and pepper.
- In a shallow dish, whisk the egg with a splash of milk.

- In another shallow dish, combine the parmesan cheese with the breadcrumbs.
- One piece at a time, dip the chicken breasts in the egg mixture, turning to coat; let excess drip off. Drip into the parmesan mix, turning to coat; shake excess.
- Put the breaded chicken into a greased 13x9-inch casserole dish; bake at 350F for about 20-25 minutes or till the center is no longer pink and the juices run clear. To check for doneness, cut a small slit in the center of 1 chicken breast using a knife; pull open to see if the meat is white and no longer pink.
- Top each chicken breast with 1 spoonful or more of pasta sauce; spread the sauce around the top of each chicken piece, sprinkle about 1 to 2 tablespoons of mozzarella cheese over the top as well.

- Return the chicken into the oven; bake for 5 minute more or until the cheese is melted. Serve warm with pasta.

Herb Roasted Pork Tenderloin

Ingredients:

- 1 1/4 pounds pork tenderloin
- 1 tablespoon olive oil
- 1 teaspoon dried oregano
- 1 teaspoon garlic powder
- 1 teaspoon ground coriander
- 1 teaspoon ground cumin
- 1/2 teaspoon ground thyme
- 1/2 teaspoon onion powder
- 1/2 teaspoon salt
- 1/4 teaspoon pepper

Directions:

- Preheat the oven to 450F.
- In a small-sized bowl, combine the garlic powder with the cumin, oregano, thyme, coriander, salt, onion powder, and pepper; set aside.
- Put the pork tenderloin roasting pan lined parchment paper or foil.
- Rub the pork tenderloin all over with seasoning mix, gently pressing so the seasoning adheres.
- Bake for about 20 to 25 minutes or till the internal temperature is 145F and the inside is slightly pink; make sure not overcook.

- Let rest for about 5 to 10 minutes so the juices redistribute. Slice at an angle and serve.

Mexican Pulled Pork

Ingredients:

4-7 pounds pork shoulder

4 cloves garlic

2 tablespoons white cooking wine

2 tablespoons salt

2 tablespoons olive oil

1/4 cup brown sugar (mix 1/4 tablespoon molasses + 1/4 cup sweetener)

1/2 teaspoon chili powder

1 teaspoon ground cumin

1 teaspoon dried oregano

1 medium onion

Pepper, to taste

Directions:

- Rinse the pork shoulder and then pat dry.
- Put the cumin, dried oregano, salt, chili powder, black pepper, olive oil, garlic, brown sugar substitute, white wine, and the onion quarter into blender or food processor; blend or process until well combined.
- Pour the cumin mix over the pork shoulder; rub the mix on every surface of the meat.

- Put the pork into a Dutch oven or into a roasting pan. Pour 2 cups water.
- Tightly cover; roast the pork at 300F for about 4 1/2 hours, turning once halfway through cooking.
- When the pork is tender and pulls away easily, increase the heat 425F, remove the lid; roast with the skin side up for another 15-20 minutes to get the skin crispy.
- When done, let rest for about 15 minutes. With 2 forks, shred the pork and pour the juices over the shredded meat.
- Serve with warm tortillas, sour cream, lime wedges, guacamole, pico or your choice of Mexican fixings.

Broiled Parmesan Tilapia

Ingredients:

2 pounds tilapia fillets

1/8 teaspoon celery salt

1/4 teaspoon ground black pepper

1/4 teaspoon garlic powder

1/4 cup fresh herbs, minced

1/4 cup butter, softened

1/2 cup Parmesan cheese, freshly grated

3 tablespoons Greek yogurt (or mayo)

Juice of 1 lemon

Salt and pepper

Zest of 1 lemon

Directions:

- Preheat the broiler.
- Grease a rimmed sheet pan with olive oil.
- In a bowl, mix the parmesan cheese, with the Greek yogurt, butter, lemon juice, and lemon zest, 1/4 teaspoon of black pepper, basil, celery salt, and onion powder; set aside.
- Rinse the tilapia and then pat dry. Lay the fillets into the prepared pan, season both sides with a little salt and pepper.

- Broil a couple of inches from the source for 2 minutes, flip, and broil for 2 minutes more.
- Remove from the oven; generously spread parmesan cheese topping over the top.
- Return to the oven; broil for another 2 minutes or till the top is golden. The fish is done when they flake easily when tested; do not overcook.

Parmesan and Cracker Crusted Tilapia
Ingredients:

1 1/2 pounds tilapia fillets (or sole), rinsed and patted dry

1 cup oyster crackers

1 tablespoon Old Bay seasoning

1 teaspoon garlic powder

1/3 cup multigrain crackers

1/3cup flat-leaf parsley

2 large eggs, beaten

2 tablespoons fresh thyme leaves (or 2 teaspoons of dried thyme leaves)

3 tablespoons fresh chives, chopped

3/4 cup Parmesan cheese

Lemon wedges, for serving

Olive oil, for frying

Salt and pepper, to taste

Splash of heavy cream or half-and-half

Whole-wheat flour, for coating

Directions:

- Preheat the oven to 200F. With a food processor, grind the multigrain crackers with the oyster crackers, parmesan cheese, thyme, chives, garlic powder, and Old Bay seasoning; transfer into a shallow bowl.
- Put the flour into a different shallow bowl. In another bowl, beat the eggs with the cream.
- Fill a large-sized skillet with 1/4-inch deep of oil; heat over medium flame/heat. Season the fish fillets with the salt and pepper.
- Coat the fish with the flour; shake off excess. Coat with the egg mix and then with the cracker crumb mix.
- Cooking 2 fillets at a time, fry the fish in the skillet for about 5 minutes, turning once while frying, until deep golden Transfer each batch into the oven to keep warm. Serve with lemon wedges.
- Freezing: Bread the fish as directed, put in freezable bags, and freeze.
- When ready to serve, transfer into the fridge and let thaw overnight.
- Cook according to directions.

Roasted Salmon Red Pepper

Ingredients:

8 pieces (4 ounces) fillets salmon

4 tablespoons soy sauce

4 tablespoons green onions, chopped

4 tablespoons balsamic vinegar (or sub rice vinegar or red wine vinegar)

3 teaspoons brown sugar

2 teaspoons crushed red pepper flakes

2 cloves garlic, minced

1/2 teaspoon salt

1/2 cup peanut oil

1 teaspoon sesame oil

1 1/2 teaspoons ground ginger

Directions:

- In a gallon Ziploc bag, put all the ingredients except for the salmon fillets; zip and shake until well combined.
- Add the salmon fillets into the marinade, seal, and marinate in the fridge for 1 hour. You can freeze the fillets at this point.

For grilling:

- Prepare the outdoor grill with coals 5 inches from the grate; lightly grease the grate.
- Grill the fish 5 inches from the coals for 10 minutes per 1 inch of thickness, measured at the thickest part, or until the fish easily flakes when tested with a fork.
- Turn the fish fillets halfway through grilling.

For roasting:

- Preheat the oven to 400F; roast for 20 minutes.

Rosemary Shrimp Scampi

Ingredients:

1 pound (about 40 large-sized) shrimp, peeled and then deveined (about 1 pound)

Cooking spray

Lemon wedges, optional

For the marinade:

1/2 teaspoon freshly ground black pepper

1/2 teaspoon red pepper flakes

2 pieces (6-inch) rosemary sprig, stems discarded and finely chopped

2 teaspoon salt

6 garlic cloves, minced

6 tablespoons fresh lemon juice

8 tablespoons olive oil

Directions:

- Combine the marinade ingredients in Ziploc bag. Add the shrimp, seal, and shake to coat.

- Put in the fridge and marinate for 30 minutes, occasionally turning the bag.
- Broil or grill the shrimps for 2 minutes each side or until pink.
- If desired, serve with lemon wedges.

Sweet and Savory Salmon

Ingredients:

2 pounds salmon

1/4 teaspoon salt

1/4 teaspoon red pepper flakes

1/4 teaspoon black pepper

1/4 cup honey

1 tablespoon thinly sliced green onion, plus more for garnish

1 tablespoon sesame oil

1 tablespoon rice vinegar

1 tablespoon freshly grated ginger

2 tablespoons reduced-sodium soy sauce

3 cloves garlic, minced

Directions:

- Inside a large-sized Ziploc bag, combine the honey with the sesame oil, soy sauce, rice vinegar, garlic, ginger, red pepper, green onion, salt, and pepper; seal and shake until combined.
- Add the salmon fillets, seal, and turn to coat. Put in the fridge and marinate for about 15 to 30 minutes, turning 1-2 times during marinating.
- Preheat the oven to 375F. Line a baking sheet with heavy-duty foil.
- Remove the salmon from the marinade; lay into the prepared baking sheet; fold up all the 4 sides of the foil.

- Pour the marinade over the salmon. Pinch the foil sides, covering the salmon completely and sealing closed, making sure to leave a little space at the top.
- Put the baking sheet in the oven; bake for about 15 to 20 minutes or till almost cooked through. Remove from the oven and open the packet.
- Turn the broiler on; broil for about 2 to 3 minutes or till slightly charred or until caramelized. Garnish with some green onions.
- Serve the salmon and the cooked sauce from the foil over brown rice.

Italian Sausage and Tortellini Soup
Ingredients:

1 can (28 ounces) tomato sauce

1 cans (14 ounces) diced tomatoes (liquid and all)

1 cup carrots, sliced (about 2-3 medium carrots)

1 cup frozen corn

1 jalapeno pepper, diced (or add to the soup whole and you can pull it out later)

1 onion, diced

1 package (16 ounces) frozen cheese multi-colored tortellini (I used Trader Joe's tortellini)

1 teaspoon Italian Seasoning

1/2 teaspoon dried basil

1/2 teaspoon ground black pepper (or more to taste)

1-2 stalks celery, sliced

16-ounce Italian sausage, crumbled and browned

2 bay leaves

2 cans (non-marinated 14 ounces) quartered artichoke hearts (liquid and all)

2 cans French Onion Soup (or 1 sautéed diced onion and 4 cups broth)

3 garlic cloves, minced

4 cups vegetable broth or chicken broth

Olive oil

Directions:

- Inside a large-sized stockpot, brown the Italian sausage over medium high heat, until cooked through.
- Add the seasonings; set aside. Wipe the pot clean.
- Put about 1 to 2 tablespoons olive oil into the pot; swirl to coat the bottom and heat over medium high heat.
- Add the celery, carrots, garlic, and onion; sauté for about 3 to 4 minutes or till soft; lightly season with salt and pepper to taste while sautéing.

- Return the cooked sausage into the pot. Add the artichoke hearts, tomato sauce, tomatoes, broth, French onion soup, corn, and the bay leaves; stir to combine and bring to a boil.
- Reduce the heat to a simmer; cook for about 15 to 20 minutes.
- Add the tortellini; cook according to the directions on the package, just a couple minutes before serving.
- Remove the bay leaves. Serve topped with parmesan cheese.

Szechuan Steak Stir-Fry

Ingredients:

1 pound steak (any kind), sliced thin, 1-2" long pieces

1 tablespoon sesame oil

1 teaspoon sugar

1/3 cup fresh cilantro, chopped

1/4 cup soy sauce, all natural

1/4 cup water

1/4 teaspoon red pepper flakes

1-2 tablespoon vegetable or peanut oil

2 garlic cloves, minced

2 tablespoons dry-roasted peanuts, chopped

2 tablespoons stir-fry sauce, all natural

2 teaspoons cornstarch

2-3 cups (about 1 small package) frozen stir-fry vegetables

Directions:

- Inside a large-sized Ziploc bag, combine the garlic cloves with the soy sauce, red pepper flakes, stir-fry sauce, and the sesame oil; seal and shake until well combined.

- Add the steak in the bag, put in the fridge, add marinate for at least 1 hour.

- In a bowl, combine the cornstarch with the water and sugar; set aside. Heat a large-sized skillet or a wok over medium-high heat.

- Add the veggies; stir-fry for about 2 to 3 minutes or till tender crisp, making sure not to overcook. Transfer into a plate.

- Add the beef and the marinade into the skillet or wok; stir-fry until the meat is cooked through, for about 1 to 2 minutes.

- Return the veggies to the pan; toss with the sauce and the meat; bring the sauce to a simmer.

- Add the cornstarch mix, continue stir-frying for 1 minute or so or until the sauce is thick. Top with the peanuts and the cilantro. Serve over cauliflower rice.

Appetizers

Sardine Spread

- Serving Size: 4
- Add up to Time: 5 min
- Prep: 5 min
- Cook: 0 min

Directions:

Crush, blend, and serve this spread in a matter of seconds! Sardines are a decent wellspring of omega-3 unsaturated fats, calcium, iron, and potassium.

Fixings:

2 3.75-ounce jars sardines without salt, depleted and crushed

2 lemons, pressed

1/2 teaspoon hot pepper sauce

1/2 container no-additional salt ketchup

Bearings:

Combine all elements for spread in a little bowl.

Fill in as a spread for 100% entire grain saltines.

Cut Tomatoes Balsamic Glaze

- Serves 2
- Serving Size: 2 cuts
- Add up to Time: 5 min
- Prep: 5 min
- Cook: 0 min

Directions:

This is an incredible canapé or nibble that you can make with fixings you as of now have in your refrigerator and storeroom.

Fixings:

1 extremely ready, extensive tomato

1 tablespoon balsamic vinegar coat

1/2 teaspoon olive oil

Headings:

Cut the tomato and mastermind 2-3 cuts on each plate. Shower with olive oil. At that point pour a lace of balsamic vinegar coat down the focal point of the cuts.

Discretionary enhancement: little saltine wafers

Crude Veggie Platter

- Serves 10

- Serving Size: 3/4 glass

- Add up to Time: 10 min

- Prep: 10 min

- Cook: 0 min

Directions:

Serve this brilliant veggie platter with one measure of hummus, bean plunge or sans fat farm dressing.

Fixings:

2 glasses carrot sticks

2 glasses celery sticks

1 glass cherry tomatoes

1 glass broccoli florets

1 glass cauliflower florets

1 glass radishes

Headings:

Peel and cut all vegetables. Mastermind them on an alluring platter with a bowl of dunk in the inside.

Cover and refrigerate until prepared to serve.

Crude Veggie Platter

- Serves 10
- Serving Size: 3/4 container
- Add up to Time: 10 min
- Prep: 10 min
- Cook: 0 min

Directions:

Serve this bright veggie platter with one measure of hummus, bean plunge or without fat farm dressing.

Fixings:

2 containers carrot sticks

2 containers celery sticks

1 glass cherry tomatoes

1 glass broccoli florets

1 glass cauliflower florets

1 glass radishes

Headings:

Peel and cut all vegetables. Mastermind them on an appealing platter with a bowl of dunk in the inside.

Cover and refrigerate until prepared to serve.

Strawberry Sparklers

- Serves 6
- Serving Size: 3-4 strawberries for every serving
- Add up to Time: 10 min
- Prep: 10 min
- Cook: 0 min

Directions:

Serve these fun strawberries for a nibble or treat.

Fixings:

1 pound crisp vast strawberries

1 glass light cream cheddar

2 tablespoons every: pistachios, almonds, dried pineapple, dried cranberries, cleaved chocolate chips

Wash strawberries under frosty, running water to expel any abundance earth. Pat them extremely dry with paper towels.

Put cream cheddar in little glass bowl, cover and microwave until delicate and warm, around 30 seconds. Mix well.

Put hacked things in little bowls.

Plunge strawberries in cream cheddar, then in one of the slashed blends. Put them on a little plate, then refrigerate to solidify the cream cheddar. Serve chilled.

You will have 1/2 measure of cream cheddar left over; hold it for another utilization. Hold sprinkle things for more sweets - they make awesome embellishments.

Tomato Pinwheels Tapas

- Serves 2
- Serving Size: 1/2 container
- Add up to Time: 5 min
- Prep: 5 min
- Cook: 0 min

Directions:

These tasty hors d'oeuvres are a sound other option to stowed potato chips.

Fixings:

1 entire wheat tortilla

2 tablespoons arranged hummus

1 hacked, ready plum tomato

1 container grape or cherry tomatoes

Bearings:

Spread the entire wheat tortilla with the hummus.

Put the diced tomatoes toward one side and roll firmly.

Cut in 1 inch pieces and organize around on a plate. Put the grape or cherry tomatoes in the inside.

Tortilla Pizza

- Serves 1
- Serving Size: 4 pieces
- Add up to Time: 10 min
- Prep: 5 min
- Cook: 5 min

Directions:

This pizza is enthusiastic about taste, yet low in calories!

Fixings:

1 entire wheat flour tortilla

1/4 container hacked broccoli tops

1/4 glass cleaved green onions

1/4 glass cut mushrooms

1/4 glass no-salt-included tomato sauce

1/4 glass diminished fat destroyed cheddar

1/4 teaspoon oregano

Headings:

Preheat broiler to 400°F.

Put tortilla on a treat plate. Beat with the sauce, broccoli, onions, and mushrooms. Sprinkle with cheddar and oregano.

Heat the pizza until cheddar is liquefied, around 5 minutes.

Cut into 4 pieces and serve hot.

Tuna Tomato Sandwich

- Serves 2
- Serving Size: 1 open-confronted sandwich
- Add up to Time: 5 min
- Prep: 5 min
- Cook: 0 min

Directions:

This delicious sandwich meets up rapidly however keeps you full for quite a long time.

Fixings:

1 6-ounce can light fish stuffed in water, depleted

1 tomato, cored and diced little

2 tablespoons without fat mayonnaise

2 containers destroyed romaine lettuce

2 cuts 100% entire wheat bread, toasted

Culinary expert's Tips:

A plate of mixed greens or a measure of vegetable soup would make a brilliant side dish for this feast.

Blend fish, tomato, and mayonnaise in a little blending dish.

Make two open-confronted sandwiches: best each cut of bread with lettuce and fish serving of mixed greens.

Crostini with Sundried Tomatoes

- Serves 8
- Serving Size: 2 cuts
- Add up to Time: 20 min
- Prep: 5 min
- Cook: 15 min

Directions:

A spread you can set aside a few minutes for a flawlessly firm and crunchy hors d'oeuvre, side dish, or nibble.

Fixings:

1 glass bubbling water

15 sun-dried tomato parts

1 garlic clove, pounded

2 tablespoons crisp basil, finely cleaved

Squeeze dark pepper

1 little baguette, cut in 1/2 inch cuts

Pour the bubbling water over the tomatoes and put aside until mellowed, around 30 minutes.

Deplete the tomatoes and coarsely hack them. Put them in a vast blending dish and include whatever is left of the fixings, aside from the bread cuts.

Preheat the stove to 350°F.

Cut the baguette and orchestrate the cuts in a solitary layer on a heating sheet. Toast in the stove until both sides are fresh.

Permit to cool and present with the sun-dried tomato spread.

Dried Fruit Plate Tapas

- Serves 8
- Serving Size: 1/2 container
- Add up to Time: 5 min
- Prep: 5 min
- Cook: 0 min

Directions:

Fixings:

1 container dried figs

1 container dried cranberries

1 container prunes

1 apple, cored and cut in wedges

Lemon wedge

Dried natural product is famous in the Mediterranean. We made a platter with figs (cut them down the middle so they look better), dried cranberries, dried plums (this is a tricky word for prunes), and apple wedges covered with lemon juice. We duped and utilized the apple wedges that are as of now cut and in packs in the supermarket.

By making these 5 little plates and masterminding them around the room you have a decent canapé spread or extraordinary nibble plates in your fridge. Utilize them for the Super Bowl or for at whatever time of year – for gatherings or after school snacks. Everybody adores the assortment!

Entrees

Antipasto Bean Salad

- Serves 4
- Serving Size: 2 containers
- Add up to Time: 15 min
- Prep: 5 min
- Cook: 10 min

Directions:

This crisp spring plate of mixed greens is exceptionally beautiful with dark beans, red leaf lettuce, radishes, and the sky is the limit from there. It is a heavenly approach to eat more vegetables.

Fixings:

6 mugs red leaf lettuce

1/4 glass nonfat Italian serving of mixed greens dressing

1 glass 3-inch celery sticks

1/2 glass cut radishes

1 15-ounce can dark beans, flushed and depleted

1 glass solidified artichoke hearts, defrosted

4 tablespoons ground Parmesan cheddar

Hurl red leaf lettuce in medium-sized bowl with dressing. Partition among 4 supper measured plates.

Orchestrate celery sticks, radishes, dark beans, and artichoke hearts in ornamental way over the highest point of the hurled lettuce. Sprinkle the highest point of each presenting with Parmesan cheddar.

Asian Chicken Vegetable Salad

- Serves 4
- Serving Size: 1 glass
- Add up to Time: 15 min
- Prep: 5 min
- Cook: 10 min

Directions:

This generous serving of mixed greens makes a filling supper.

Fixings:

1 pound solidified panfry vegetables

2 tablespoons light soy sauce

1 tablespoon sesame oil

1 cup cooked chicken bosom, skinless, cubed

8 mugs prepared to-serve spinach clears out

3 tablespoons red wine vinegar

Daintily shower a substantial non-stick skillet with vegetable cooking splash and warmth over medium-high warmth. Sauté the vegetables until fresh delicate and warmed through, around 5 minutes.

Asian Style Flounder

- Serves 4
- Serving Size: 4 ounces
- Add up to Time: 15 min
- Prep: 5 min
- Cook: 10 min

Directions:

Flaky fumble with an Asian style is anything but difficult to make in one heating dish and in 10 minutes.

Fixings:

1 glass cleaved green onion

1 tablespoon ground ginger

1 tablespoon minced garlic

2 tablespoons light soy sauce

2 teaspoons sesame oil

16 ounces crisp fumble

4 glasses crude spinach

Preheat broiler to 350°F.

Put spinach in heating dish and after that top with fish and whatever remains of the fixings. Prepare the fish until done, around 10 minutes.

Asian Wrap

- Serves 4
- Serving Size:
- Add up to Time: 10 min
- Prep: 5 min
- Cook: 5 min

Directions:

Like panfry in a hurry, this solid wrap is made with tofu, veggies, and chestnut rice.

Fixings:

1/2 container cubed firm tofu

2 tablespoons lite soy sauce

2 teaspoons nectar

1 teaspoon sesame oil

1/2 teaspoon sesame seeds

1/2 teaspoon five flavor flavoring

1 container broccoli florets, washed with water

1/2 container cut carrots

1 container cut mushrooms

2 containers cooked chestnut rice

4 entire wheat tortillas

Marinate the tofu with the soy sauce, nectar, sesame oil, sesame seeds, and five flavor flavoring in a little bowl and put aside.

Avocado Spinach Sandwich

- Serves 1
- Serving Size:
- Add up to Time: 5 min
- Prep: 5 min
- Cook: 0 min

Directions:

This brisk sandwich will keep you full for a considerable length of time!

Fixings:

2 cuts 100% entire wheat bread

1 teaspoon light mayonnaise

1/4 glass avocado, cut

1 tomato, cut

1 glass prepared to-serve crude spinach

1/4 glass cut red onion

Toast bread and spread with mayonnaise. Put spinach leaves on one side and top with avocado, tomato, and onion cuts. Put the other cut of bread on top and appreciate.

Baked Fish with Rainbow Salsa

- Serves 4

- Serving Size: 1 container
- Add up to Time: 30 min
- Prep: 10 min
- Cook: 20 min

Directions:

This dish is tasty and brilliant and incredible for any mid-year dinner. For best outcomes, utilize a light fleshed fish, for example, Mahi, struggle, scrod, grouper or haddock.

Fixings:

4-ounce filets of fish, new or defrosted

1 teaspoon paprika

4 tablespoons water

Salsa:

1/2 container diced pineapple, new or canned

1/2 container diced mangoes or peaches

1/4 container diced green onion

1/2 container diced chime peppers

1/2 container diced ready tomatoes

Juice of 1 lime

1 diced jalapeno

2 tablespoons cleaved new cilantro

Preheat stove to 350°F.

Put the fish filets on a preparing container with water so they are spread equally separated.

Sprinkle the highest points of the fish with the paprika. Prepare until the fish is done - when it pieces separated and is fork delicate, around 15-20 minutes.

In the meantime, put the elements for the salsa in a medium-sized bowl and blend well. Serve each filet of fish with 1/2 measure of salsa on each.

Baked Potatoes Primavera

- Serves 4
- Serving Size: 1 potato
- Add up to Time: 20 min
- Prep: 5 min
- Cook: 15 min

Directions:

Prepared potatoes can get negative criticism, however it truly all relies on upon what you best them with. This dish highlights an assortment of veggies and herbs, and makes a snappy, generous dinner.

Fixings:

4 medium potatoes

4 mugs solidified blended vegetables

1-1/4 mugs nonfat sharp cream

1/2 teaspoon dried oregano

1/2 teaspoon dried basil

Dark pepper to taste

Penetrate every potato a few circumstances with a fork. Microwave on high until delicate, around 3-4 minutes for each potato. Steam blended vegetables until hot. Blend the acrid cream with the herbs and pepper. Part the potato in the inside and load with steamed veggies. Best with harsh cream and serve hot.

Barbecued Portobello Burger

- Serves 4
- Serving Size: 1 burger
- Add up to Time: 15 min
- Prep: 5 min
- Cook: 10 min

Directions:

Portobello mushrooms are cooked delicate in tart hot grill sauce and served inside hard French-style rolls.

Fixings:

2 extensive crisp Portobello mushrooms, cut in 1/4 inch cuts

1/2 container grill sauce

4 French style rolls

2 containers dim green lettuce

1 extensive tomato, cut thin

4 1/4-inch cuts red onion

Put Portobello mushroom cuts and grill sauce in expansive shallow microwaveable holder. Cover and microwave until delicate, around 3 or 4 minutes.

Warm comes in toaster broiler or stove, then cut down the middle on a level plane.

Assemble burger with Portobello mushroom cuts on base and lettuce, tomato, and onion on top. Top with move tops.

BBQ Vegetable Pockets

- Serves 4
- Serving Size: 1 parcel
- Add up to Time: 30 min
- Prep: 10 min
- Cook: 20 min

Directions:

A pocket brimming with delectable and nutritious veggies that is easy to make.

Fixings:

4 bits of aluminum thwart (12 inch squares)

1 glass diced onion

1 glass cut carrots

1/2 glass cut mushrooms

1 glass cooked (or canned) dark beans, depleted

2 mugs diced zucchini

1/2 glass low-sodium ketchup

1/2 glass arranged salsa

1 tablespoon vinegar

1 tablespoon cocoa sugar

Preheat broiler to 375°F.

Lay 4 bits of aluminum thwart out on counter. Partition vegetables and beans between each bit of thwart, putting them in the middle.

Blend ketchup, salsa, vinegar and cocoa sugar. Put 2-1/2 tablespoons of sauce over each heap of veggies. Overlap corners of thwart askew and seal well. Heat for 15-20 minutes.

Expel from broiler and permit to sit for a moment; serve hot. Take mind when opening hot parcels.

Bean Burrito Wrap

- Serves 6
- Serving Size:
- Add up to Time: 5 min
- Prep: 5 min
- Cook: 0 min

Directions:

This formula is a wrap! It is so natural to wrap beans, lettuce, and veggies in a tortilla. You can cut it into 1-inch pinwheels for an incredible introduction that elements chomp measure pieces.

Fixings:

1 low-fat, entire wheat flour tortilla

1/2 glass low-fat refried beans (canned), warmed

1 little cleaved tomato

1/4 glass destroyed lettuce

1 tablespoon sans fat harsh cream

Dash hot sauce

Spread the refried beans on the tortilla. Beat with tomatoes, lettuce, harsh cream, and hot sauce. Move up into a wrap and serve.

Conclusion

I hope that this book could help you to begin on healthy and smarter prepared Journey. You now have the complete guide to plan and make great dishes for your family.

This book is intended to enable you by giving fundamental step by step preparing methods with the best formulas to help you make solid healthy lifestyle and felling Awesome.

If you received value from this book, then I did like to ask you for a favor would you be kind enough to leave a review for this book on Amazon.

Johnny Markus

http://howdoyoubulkup.com

Printed in Great Britain
by Amazon